THINK LIKE A BRAIN

A New Map for Treating Minds That Don't Fit the Manual

DR. STEVEN RONDEAU

Think Like a Brain
A New Map for Treating Minds That Don't Fit the Manual

Written by Steven Rondeau

Design and cover art by Peaceful Profits.

Paperback ISBN: 978-1-967587-66-7
eBook ISBN: 978-1-967587-67-4

Dedication

To my wife, Mary, and our two children, Jerome and Max, who teach me something new every day. Thank you for your endless love and support and for sharing in our family's own journey with brain assessments, which have given me insights as a father, spouse, and clinician that I never could have gained any other way.

To the incredible families we've been blessed to work with, whose openness and trust have helped us all understand so much more about how these pieces come together. We're still learning, and we're so much better walking this path together.

There are too many of you to name, but thank you to my mentors throughout this journey. Each conversation, each lesson, each moment of guidance has shaped not just my work, but who I am.

To the courageous providers who are already transforming the system, choosing every day to be heroes for their patients by embracing what's possible beyond guesswork. Your dedication gives me hope and keeps me going.

And to the future we're creating together: a world where mental health care is filled with hope instead of confusion, where every person gets the care their beautiful, unique brain deserves, and where families never have to endure endless trial and error again.

The best truly is yet to come.

Table of Contents

Introduction

Sophie's Story

Throughout this book, we'll join a struggling young girl named Sophie—a vivacious child who turns into a sullen teenager, complete with harsh mood swings, dropping grades, and helpless parents. We'll watch as she cycles through therapists, psychiatrists, and other health care providers; each step of the journey providing answers, but none of these answers providing lasting solutions. By the time Sophie arrives at my clinic, her parents will have spent thousands of dollars on medications, therapy sessions, and potentially more esoteric treatments, while Sophie herself feels trapped, alone, and hopeless.

As much as this is Sophie's story, it's also a story about her father, Mark. He's a psychiatrist with decades of experience under his belt. He's worked with many cases like Sophie's and is intimately familiar with the psychiatric system of diagnosing and treating mental illness.

But through firsthand experience, he'll start to realize that the field he cares so deeply about may be fundamentally flawed. He'll watch her struggle with a cocktail of medications that seem to sometimes do more harm than good, and watch her withdraw deeper and deeper without any real hope of getting better.

He'll realize that what he thought were objective tests aren't; instead they're the result of a subjective system that groups together symptoms without any thought to their underlying cause. And, worse, he'll directly see the damage this approach does, both to patients and their families. He'll watch his daughter collect diagnostic labels like collectible tokens to no avail.

The good news for both Mark and Sophie is that hope is on the horizon: Many psychiatrists have recognized the concerns surrounding their profession and are exploring novel treatments and diagnostic tools. At the same time, patients want answers when a treatment doesn't work, which happens frequently since in psychiatry, a diagnosis doesn't necessarily correlate to a treatment outcome. All across the country, in practices, clinics, and inpatient facilities, we're seeing the paradigm shift happen in real time and are excited at what the future holds for people like Sophie, her parents, and her health care providers.

Everyone knows a Sophie. This book is about how the system has failed people like Sophie, and what we can do to prevent it happening to others just like her. Sophie's story is not unique—there are systemic problems in psychiatry that make the process of getting treatment for mental health a gamble. And it's a gamble that is, too often, a losing one.

Despite the similarities to many patients and providers our clinic has worked with, Sophie's story is a work of fiction. Names, characters, and incidents either are used fictitiously. Any resemblance to actual events or persons, living or dead, is entirely coincidental.

The Core Problem Psychiatry Faces Today

Psychiatry, like any other medical profession, faces pressures and challenges. Provider burnout from a massive increase in patients and a lack of providers are both concerns that plague most of medicine in the United States. But psychiatry also faces a unique challenge: a lack of consistent delivery.

Psychiatrists have an incredibly difficult job of sifting through symptoms to arrive at a diagnosis and treatment plan. This book will describe how the biggest challenges in modern psychiatry arose, why they perpetuate, and what the future holds.

A lack of consistency in the diagnosis process, and the resulting lack of consistency in the treatment, is due to the subjective nature of psychiatry. In most other fields of medicine, there's a clear pathway from diagnosis to first-line treatment, second-line treatment and so on. Of course, in psychiatry there are guidelines, but they rely on subjective judgments and family history with little basis in the biological cause of the concern.

The root of the issue is the diagnostic tool that all psychiatrists refer to: the Diagnostic and Statistical Manual of Mental Disorders (DSM). Mental health practitioners use it to provide patients displaying symptoms with a label—thus providing patients with a diagnosis and the treatment that goes along with it, even though evidence shows that a diagnosis is not a reliable treatment predictor. It overpathologizes and underemphasizes the strengths that come with deviations from the norm while neglecting the sheer diversity of conditions such as depression and attention deficit hyperactivity disorder (ADHD).

A parent notices that their 11-year-old child is disorganized, has difficulty with their homework, and is emotionally volatile, and decides to take them to a psychiatrist. Most will agree that the child has ADHD, but their treatment recommendations may vary from stimulants to talk therapy or even dietary changes. These recommendations are based on the subjective experiences of each provider, and because they aren't rooted in biology, it is a guessing game as to which treatment will be successful.

While changes are starting to happen—such as the rise of neuropsychology, the interest in psychedelics, and the shift towards objective testing such as the quantitative electroencephalogram (qEEG) that measures brain activity—people are still struggling to get the help they need. In my professional opinion, we need to accelerate the shift away from subjective approaches toward objective testing that can more reliably predict treatment response variability.

Why I'm Writing This Book

I didn't set out to write a book—I set out to solve a problem.

Providers have the best intentions for their patients, but much of psychiatry relies on guesswork, leading to less than ideal outcomes for many patients. I want to change the way providers and patients view mental health, largely by doing qEEG testing, which objectively measures brain activity.

People are a mix of unique traits and tendencies that respond differently to various environments. What we've found is that different qEEG brain patterns predictably map a set of tendencies and characteristics, and we can use these brain patterns to inform the support and conditions certain people need to thrive.

Every person's brain patterns dictate how they assimilate in their environment. They act as a sort of filter through which we interpret experiences and environments. I've witnessed many children who are assumed to be spoiled or manipulative that are, in fact, extraordinarily gifted but deeply misunderstood. And because the current psychiatric model does not support the complexity of the interaction of these biological traits and the environment, the solution is often medication, which may not always be the best option.

A husky has a set of traits and characteristics that equip it to thrive in cold, harsh conditions where it has one job—to pull a sled with its pack. If you put that same husky in the desert, it will be lethargic and slow. If you put the same husky in a small house, it will become destructive because it doesn't have any outlet to do its job. The husky and its characteristics haven't changed—but its environment has.

While the ultimate goal is to change how psychiatry is practiced and mental health conditions understood, there's also the goal of helping people *before* they reach their breaking point. Many people come to us after they've tried seemingly everything, saying "Well, let's just try this thing, and if it works—great. But, I'm sort of out of energy, and don't have anything left in the tank." I don't want to be a net for people who only have 10% of their energy left; I want to catch people in the beginning to help them avoid the struggle to find a treatment that works for their particular set of biological traits. In an ideal world, we'd prevent the occurrence of symptoms by identifying a person's strengths through brain patterns, rather than by trial and error, and building nurturing environments where their negative aspects don't manifest and maladaptive coping mechanisms aren't necessary.

Unfortunately, at the moment very few patients will ask their providers for objective tests, and that's why we need the science and the books; we need people speaking about this so that it just becomes the standard of care.

I want to prevent people from going through this dysfunctional trial and error system, eroding their own confidence and their own mental health. I especially want to prevent the fights between the parents and the children and the fights between the parents and their partner—many of which are caused because there isn't an understanding of the problems facing modern psychiatry. At the same time, providers have this pressure on them to help their patients get better, and their job is made more difficult because they have to guess. Their patient's successes are reliant on their interpretations.

My first specialty was autism and viewing it through a medical lens. I would attend conferences with researchers presenting about laboratory biomarkers from blood, stool samples, and urine, and looking for an objective test for autism. I then incorporated working with children suffering from pediatric autoimmune neuropsychiatric disorders associated with streptococcal infections (PANDAS)—again, a medical condition that manifests as a psychiatric one—and children with Dravet Syndrome, a medication-resistant form of childhood epilepsy.

All of my experiences meant that I've always viewed mental health through an objective medical lens, where instead of trying to treat symptoms, you look for the underlying causes of symptoms. And my interest in qEEG analysis stemmed from that worldview.

I was working in a rehabilitation center for young adults who struggled with substance abuse, where I noticed a correlation in certain tendencies and brain patterns observed in qEEG testing. This initial observation, combined with my medical view, set me on the path that led to the development of a qEEG testing facility and working with mental health providers. And through these experiences, I've witnessed firsthand the challenges facing mental health care.

I'm writing this book so that people don't get to a place of despair because nothing they've tried has worked.

By conducting over 50,000 brain scans in the last decade, we've learned about the variance of mental health. If we continue to practice psychiatry the way we're practicing now, and continue to look for new treatments for mental health conditions without looking at the biology and without objective biomarker-driven testing, we're going to continue to have the same problems.

That's what's currently happening with psychedelics that are being studied to help medication-resistant depression, suicidality, post-traumatic stress disorder (PTSD), and other conditions that are historically very hard to treat. But these treatments just added to the pool of options already available, and while they have unique mechanisms of action, simply using these treatments indiscriminately without objective testing will continue to provide the same outcomes. When I mention objective testing, I want to be clear that I don't mean symptom rating scales (more on that in later chapters). Rather, we need to be precise about what we're doing so that we can be sure that the diagnosis can lead to a predictably and consistently successful treatment outcome.

Dr. Steven Rondeau has spent over two decades developing objective approaches to mental health assessment through his work with partner clinics worldwide. His company, Axon EEG Solutions, has analyzed countless brain patterns, revealing the limitations of diagnostic labeling and the promise of objective neurological understanding.

Providing a Fresh Perspective

I am not a psychiatrist—I have a background in developmental pediatrics and naturopathic medicine, which some in psychiatry may dismiss. However, naturopathic medicine has a strong focus on identifying root causes, pattern recognition, a deep understanding of biological systems, and treating the whole rather than palliative care (managing symptoms). This has shaped how I see mental health—not as a set of checkboxes, but as a complex interplay of biology, environment, and individual characteristics.

Because I'm an outsider, I can see the flaws in the current psychiatric model clearly: The DSM isn't just outdated—it's actively holding us back.

In 2010, as I moved into collaborative work with clinicians of all stripes, I was surprised to see how few mental health providers were doing any type of objective testing. They didn't rely on lab tests or brain function assessments, but focused instead on checklists, rating scales and clinical experience. While these have their place in psychiatric practice, they do not provide any type of biological context to the patient's condition. Even the most well-intentioned treatment plans were based on assumptions, not objective data.

I will never claim to have all the answers, but I have the data, experience, and urgency to start this conversation. My credentials speak for themselves—I have published research, contributed to book chapters, mentored countless clinicians, been involved with over 50,000 qEEG tests (likely more but I've lost count), and worked with tens of thousands of patients showing a wide range of symptom presentations.

This book isn't about completely replacing the DSM, which has given us the language of psychiatry we use today. But rather, building on this foundation, we are now in a position to change the paradigm of diagnosis and treatment with objective testing opening the door to better understanding, diagnosing, and treatment of mental health conditions.

This book also isn't anti-medication either. There are plenty of effective drugs that can help people with mental health issues. Rather, my concern is that medication is prescribed indiscriminately. Surprising to many even in the field, a definitive mental health diagnosis doesn't correlate to a positive treatment outcome (read that again). Just because you get a depression diagnosis doesn't mean that a medication like Zoloft™ will work. My argument is that we need precision in the form of objective testing, which examines the organ we are professing to treat and thus allows providers to help their patients more effectively.

Whether you're someone suffering from a mental health condition, a family member or friend seeing a loved one suffer, or a clinician who is frustrated with the current DSM-based model of psychiatry, this book is for you. There is a *better way*: Once you begin to integrate objective brain testing, you won't be able to look at mental health the same way again.

Chapter 1

The Guessing Game

Sophie's Story

Growing up, Sophie loved spending time outdoors with her friends. Even during her tweens, she was easygoing and friendly and did exceptionally well at school. But around the time Sophie turned 15, that all changed; she started rejecting her friends, her grades gradually dropped, and she was constantly snapping at her parents and siblings. She spent more and more time alone in her room, watching videos and scrolling through social media.

Sophie's dad, Mark, was a psychiatrist and he had witnessed similar things happen before. However, he was also reluctant to start taking action until he was certain that it wasn't just teenage hormones.

When Mark found Sophie sobbing in the bathroom, he knew it was time to take action. Mark booked a session with one of the top-regarded psychiatrists in his area who specialized in adolescent mental health—Dr. Chen. He hoped that they could get some clarity and chart a way forward to get Sophie's life back on track.

After a thorough 90-minute evaluation and consultation, Sophie's new psychiatrist diagnosed her with major depressive disorder (F32.9), and recommended sertraline with cognitive behavioral therapy—standard of care with the label. Mark was impressed with Dr. Chen's methodology; she used validated questionnaires, considered differential diagnoses (probable causes), and applied her years of experience to arrive at the likely diagnosis and treatment.

Mark was relieved—a diagnosis meant a solution, he thought. But Sophie didn't get better; in fact, she got worse. Her mood swings intensified, and there were days where she couldn't get out of bed. "I feel like a zombie," she told her parents one day. When she did manage to get up, she struggled to concentrate and her grades continued to decline. She stopped seeing her friends and ended up even more alone than before.

Over the next three years, Sophie saw dozens of specialists, received two additional labels—generalized anxiety disorder (F41.9) and, later, ADHD (F90.9) due to her academic decline and inability to concentrate—and cycled through different medications based on her new labels, none of which provided much relief. Not only did these treatments fail, many actively made her feel worse. "Am I so broken that medicine can't fix me?" she wondered as her life fell to pieces around her. Her father was in a similar state, wondering why the practices that he relied on and that he used on his own patients weren't working for Sophie. Was he perhaps too close to the problem?

Every provider Sophie saw truly felt that they were helping her recover, and Mark couldn't detect any shortcomings in their approaches. They all applied best practices, and he agreed with their reasoning and suggestions. So why wasn't Sophie getting better?

The truth is that it wasn't Sophie who was broken—the psychiatric standard of care that relied on subjective diagnosis and treatment is at fault. In this chapter, we'll examine how psychiatry is fundamentally different from other medical fields and what this difference means for providers, their patients and their loved ones, and society at large.

The Great Gamble: Subjectivity in Psychiatry

Every year, my men's hockey team and I make the pilgrimage to Las Vegas, and I always look forward to it. I love the camaraderie, the energy of the city, and the tournaments we compete in. But what I don't enjoy, and what surprises my teammates, are the games of chance that Las Vegas is ostensibly built on.

I've never liked gambling. The house always wins, and I refuse to play rigged games, especially when every aspect of the casino is designed to entice you to play—from the maze-like layout, the lack of windows and clocks, and the constant sensory overload.

Ironically, I see a lot of parallels between gambling in Vegas and the modern psychiatric system. I know that this is a provocative statement, and I can already hear providers telling me that I am wrong. But that's the point—the psychiatric system is so encompassing, so entrenched that you may not even *notice* that you're in a casino at all.

Throughout this book, I'll talk about how modern mental health care traps experts and professionals into making critical treatment decisions based on a fluctuating subjective set of symptoms and subjective interpretation of the symptoms, including semantics (one may describe their symptoms as anxiety or racing thoughts and another as cognitive overwhelm, for example) instead of what's actually going on in the patient's brain. In this chapter, I'll look at the subjective underpinnings of the entire field and how they influence both diagnostic labels and treatment selection. The next chapter will then focus on the DSM itself and how it normalizes and promotes a diagnostic and treatment paradigm that is ultimately harmful to providers, patients, and their families.

Subjectivity involves making a judgment based on personal *beliefs* or *feelings* rather than facts.

Objectivity involves making a judgment based on facts *without* the input of personal beliefs or feelings.

In most medical fields, diagnosing a condition is typically an objective task based on the principle of *test-confirm-treat.* In this process, there are systematic steps that follow each other and rely on quantifiable data, starting with identifying the symptoms that prompt an investigation and testing. These tests produce objective data points that are used to identify a condition, and additional tests may be used to further confirm the diagnosis or to refine treatment options. Finally, testing is also done at the end of treatment to confirm that the condition has been successfully dealt with.

In more complex cases, the doctor may need to exercise a bit of subjectivity, basing their diagnosis on previous experience and reading between the lines of the patient's description of their symptoms and feelings as well as relying on test results. But the core foundation of the process remains the same: get objective data using reliable tests to get to a diagnosis and use these tests to determine the efficacy of the treatment.

Unlike other medical fields, psychiatry doesn't have many objective tests and is the only specialty that doesn't test the organ it treats—the brain. Instead, the practitioner relies on patient self-reports, clinical observations, and standardized questionnaires; psychiatry is trying to explain something without directly examining the problem. As opposed to the traditional *test-confirm-treat* paradigm, psychiatry relies on the *categorize-hope-adjust* model. In fact, response to treatment is often the only confirmation of the diagnosis, with the patients acting as an n=1 experiment.

> An n=1 experiment consists of a single patient as the sole target of the study. It allows clinicians to extensively investigate the efficacy and consequences of different interventions for that patient.

This approach is fraught with problems. Answers tend to be subjective, both from the patient's viewpoint and from the psychiatrist's perspective (they may say to the patient, "rate your mood," "how bad is your sleep," or "tell me the level of your anxiety"). While questionnaires can help make questions more standard, the psychiatrist will still need to decide whether a patient's "I'm very worried all the time" warrants a four-out-of-five or five-out-of-five on an anxiety scale.

And to complicate things further, psychiatry has plenty of examples where symptoms overlap; both depression and anxiety include sleep disturbances, fatigue, and concentration problems.[1] Similarly, trauma, general anxiety, and sensory processing concerns all lead to disproportionate feelings of dread and fear. So how does a provider distinguish between the two?

Another major concern is that the diagnosis does not directly correlate to treatment outcomes. In fact, many meta-analyses have highlighted that psychiatric treatment is like an artform that relies on trial and error.[2]

When you take your car to a mechanic, you would expect them to plug it into a computer, run some tests, and maybe troubleshoot with a book while physically looking at your car before saying "OK, I think this is the issue."

What you wouldn't expect is for them to listen to you describe the issue and then begin to start changing parts without troubleshooting or running a test. So why is this the standard of practice in mental health?

---

1 Zbozinek, T. D., Rose, R. D., Wolitzky-Taylor, K. B., Sherbourne, C., Sullivan, G., Stein, M. B., Roy-Byrne, P. P., & Craske, M. G. (2012). Diagnostic overlap of generalized anxiety disorder and major depressive disorder in a primary care sample. *Depression and Anxiety*, *29*(12), 1065–1071. https://doi.org/10.1002/da.22026

2 McMahon, F. J., (2014). Prediction of treatment outcomes in psychiatry—where do we stand? *Dialogues in Clinical Neuroscience*, *16*(4), 455–464. https://doi.org/10.31887/DCNS.2014.16.4/fmcmahon

In 2008, I vividly remember sitting down with a psychiatrist, and I asked them, "How do you know what treatment your patient needs?" And they replied, "Well, we just listen to the patient, read their intake, and put the story together—when their story makes sense, we see which diagnosis most closely aligns with it. Then, based on that information, we do the treatment for that diagnosis." Imagine what you would do if your mechanic told you that they're replacing the entire engine, because the car's symptoms align with an engine problem, without doing any further testing. To be clear, this isn't a flaw with that *one* clinician; it is a reflection of how the *entire* system functions.

Every step of the process is riddled with subjectivity and holes. Even if the diagnosis is correct, treatment response can vary dramatically between patients. Two patients with the same diagnosis may receive the same prescription and have completely opposite reactions, with one getting better while the other continues to spiral.

Why Has Psychiatry Remained So Subjective?

Psychiatry is not alone in being based in subjectivity. For the longest time, most medical practice was based on concepts like miasmas, spirits, and vague feelings that were intangible and unmeasurable. Doctors would rely only on patient's self-reporting and reach conclusions based on guesses and speculation rather than the scientific method and objective testing.

Nearly all medical fields have moved on from this way of thinking. Fields as notoriously difficult to study like cancer use objective testing as the primary way of making a diagnosis. Elevated levels of proteins such as CA27.29 or CA15-3 can be a clear warning sign of breast cancer, which can then be confirmed with modern imaging techniques and physical biopsies—techniques that, again, look directly and objectively at the organ being treated.

Even fields like pain management, neurology, and gastroenterology, which tend to rely on subjective symptom descriptions, have adopted biomarker-driven tests and diagnostic methods such as stool-based markers in gastroenterology, and magnetic resonance imaging (MRI) in neurology.

Only psychiatry continues to operate on a checklist that has few objective criteria, and when psychiatrists have tried to do objective testing in the past, it hasn't held water. For example, the neurotransmitter theory (that serotonin or other chemical imbalances in the brain cause mental health issues) has essentially been debunked,[3] leaving psychiatrists in doubt as to what actually causes conditions like depression or anxiety and making the field trepidatious about other studies into the biological causes of mental illness.

But is this enough to explain why psychiatry has remained resolutely and steadfastly subjective?

---

3 Moncrieff, J., Cooper, R. E., Stockmann, T., et al. (2023). The serotonin theory of depression: a systematic umbrella review of the evidence. *Molecular Psychiatry*, *28*, 3243–3256.

A **biomarker** is a biological characteristic or molecule that acts as a functional indicator that a biological process is working normally or is not working well. For instance, blood glucose levels are a biomarker for how well the body processes sugar, and having a high blood glucose level can indicate a disease state—diabetes. Clinicians use biomarkers to diagnose conditions but also to measure how well a patient *responds* to treatment.

At the root of this subjectivity is that the brain is admittedly challenging to test. It is highly dynamic and interconnected—memory centers interact with the executive function center, which interacts with the default mode network, etc. And measuring how all of these working parts talk to each other is extremely difficult.

Compare this to the heart; it has valves going in and valves going out, and it's pretty easy to measure its function, either through echocardiograms, electrocardiograms, blood pressure tests, or MRI. The same applies to the liver, kidneys, lungs, eyes, muscles, and joints: These are all things that are measurable with numbers and tests. But when you get into the nuances of the brain, it's significantly more complicated.

For decades, psychiatry has operated on the assumption that mental illness was caused by chemical imbalances in the brain and that adjusting neurotransmitters like serotonin or dopamine could fix conditions like depression and anxiety. However, a landmark study published in 2023[4] challenged the simple reductionist theory of serotonin imbalance as a cause of

4 Ibid.

depression. If the neurotransmitter theory has failed to guide depression treatment accurately, what's next?

And even if the neurotransmitter theory is correct in some instances and chemical imbalances can predict diagnoses and treatment outcomes for certain conditions, measuring these compounds accurately is almost impossible. The most reliable way is through testing spinal fluid, which is a challenging procedure for the patient and not something routinely performed. An alternative is urine analysis, but these findings almost never correlate with spinal fluid measurements or central brain chemistry. All of this leads to the question: If we produce most of our serotonin in our gut, is what you're measuring in the urine really reflective of what is found in the brain?

Another issue is that the language around what people are experiencing mentally is difficult to pinpoint and ambiguous in terms of how they experience it in their environment. Trying to say exactly how sad or how distracted they are; that's much harder to quantify, even with a checklist. Asking a patient to rate their anxiety or sadness on a scale of one to ten is akin to measuring the warmth of a hug with a thermometer.

Many people struggle with anxiety, but it is surprisingly easy to confuse anxiety with feeling overwhelmed. A patient may be feeling extremely stressed and constantly worried because they are overwhelmed at work. If they go to a provider, it's likely they will receive an anxiety diagnosis based on the symptoms of dread, elevated heart rate, and potential avoidance behaviors. But in reality, the patient doesn't have an anxiety disorder, and treatments aimed at anxiety disorders won't treat their underlying issue, namely that they are overwhelmed and stressed.

The difference isn't just semantic—these differences will show up as distinct brain patterns even though they present the same from a symptoms perspective. Even worse, the treatment for anxiety and overwhelm are completely different, and getting it wrong on the assessment side could lead to the patient's symptoms getting worse.

How Subjectivity Affects Psychiatric Diagnoses and Treatment

Diagnosis

Psychiatrists, much more so than other health care practitioners, have to lean on their personal experience when diagnosing conditions regardless of whether they've been in the field for a day or a decade. Instead of being able to confirm their diagnosis with an objective test, they have to use subjective checklists, previous clinical experience, and pattern recognition to arrive at a conclusion.

The pressure is extremely high to get it right, especially as there are some diagnoses, like bipolar disorder, narcissistic personality disorder, and schizophrenia, that come with significant stigma.

However, studies show that getting it right is extremely difficult. A recent UK study found that when cases for 441 people with a recent diagnosis of major depressive disorder were reviewed, 15% did not meet the criteria for that condition (or any mood disorder), while 30% actually had a different condition, bipolar disorder.[5]

> **Heterogeneity** is the term for a wide or diverse range of characteristics—for example, variations in eye, skin, or hair color in humans.

When I was mentoring, I had a group of psychiatrists reviewing brain scans. I tried to instill in them that not only does their typical reductionistic model fall short and limit the heterogeneity within the diagnosis, it also doesn't highlight any of the *strengths* of that condition. Children with ADHD can manifest the condition in many different ways, and the treatment for each of these children can be very different. Also, children with ADHD tend to be extremely creative and passionate about things to which they are interested. People with depression are more often empathetic and emotionally sensitive to the needs of others. And it's important to always highlight that a diagnosis isn't a label, but a description of certain observable characteristics.

The absence of objectivity in psychiatry also leads to concerns about whether diagnoses are consistent across cultures. Are psychiatric conditions universal: Does a depressed person in China reflect the same symptoms and outcomes as someone in Chile, or are they dependent on cultural factors? Studies

5 Martin-Key, N.A., Olmert T., Barton-Owen, G., et al. (2021). The Delta study - prevalence and characteristics of mood disorders in 924 individuals with low mood: Results of the World Health Organization composite International diagnostic interview (CIDI). *Brain Behaviour,*11, Article e02167.

show that culture and context are vital considerations during psychiatric diagnoses, and this is often exacerbated when patients are from different backgrounds than their providers.[6] Even when accounting for behavioral and demographic risk factors, white children are more likely to be diagnosed with ADHD than their Black, Hispanic/Latino and Asian peers in the United States.[7]

Providers can also fall into the trap of circular logic: When a patient responds to a treatment the diagnosis is thus confirmed, but if they don't respond, the diagnosis doesn't routinely change; however, the treatment does. This is like reading a generic fortune cookie message and saying "Oh wow, this thing is speaking to me!" even though the saying could be interpreted in 20 different ways. This type of circular logic is a clear example of confirmation bias when we interpret evidence to support our existing beliefs.

In a lot of ways, this type of subjective thinking can promote biases and reinforce existing beliefs, similar to how people find meaning in broad statements and categories. We've all fallen into the trap of thinking, *Well, I've just done such a Taurus thing*, or *I'm an ENTJ on the Myers-Briggs, which means I have to be extroverted*, and putting ourselves into neat pigeonholes. However, as double-blind studies into astrology show, these meanings may not always have a strong basis in reality.[8]

6 Alarcon, R. D. (2013). Culture, cultural factors and psychiatric diagnosis: Review and projections. *World Psychiatry*, 8: 131–139.

7 Shi Y., Hunter Guevara L. R., Dykhoff H. J., et al. (2021). Racial disparities in diagnosis of attention-deficit/hyperactivity disorder in a US national birth cohort. *JAMA Network Open*, 4, Article e210321.

8 Carlson, S. (1985). A double-blind test of astrology. *Nature*, 318, 419–425.

It's human nature to want to see patterns and organize everything into neat categories. Unfortunately, relying on subjectivity when assigning something as important as labels means that it can often end up being a self-fulfilling prophecy, like reading your star sign and saying, "Okay, this is you. Now go live your life based on the fact that you're a Scorpio." This is relatively harmless or entertaining when we're talking about star signs, but can have serious implications when mental health becomes involved.

Treatment

The subjectivity problem doesn't just affect diagnosis; it also influences treatment. Treatment choices are also often subjective, with some providers preferring therapy or nonmedical interventions, while others choosing medication as the first option.

There is a temptation to want to go into a reductionistic label model because mental health professionals are trained to think, "When I know the *label*, then I know the corresponding treatment," even though evidence shows that a *diagnosis is not a predictor of treatment outcome.*[9] It can be incredibly difficult to unlearn that approach—especially when it works effectively in other fields of medicine.

In a lot of cases, mental health diagnosis is a cascade of so many other events from school services to the psychology aisle in the bookstore to the therapist's office. However, studies have found that the diagnosis code has *little to no value* in terms of

9 Poirot, M.G., et al. (2024). Treatment response prediction in major depressive disorder using multimodal MRI and clinical data: Secondary analysis of a randomized clinical trial. *American Journal of Psychiatry,181*(3), 223–233.

predicting how people respond to treatment. People manifest their symptoms differently and they respond to treatment differently; this heterogeneity is currently not accounted for in the modern psychiatric model.

If we're using a reductionistic model based on subjectivity to measure mental health, that isn't much better than going to the health food store and picking a supplement at random and saying, "I feel anxious a lot, so I'll go down the anxiety aisle. And because I'm anxious, I'm reluctant to ask for help; I'm just going to go and try to do this on my own. And there's all these different formulas, but I don't really know what a lot of them do—some are uppers, some are downers, some calm you, and some you take at night, and I don't know which ones are going to work." That's how psychiatry currently operates. It's not that the options don't work, but that without a clear map of what's wrong, you're hoping you grab the right bottle for your flavor, or phenotype as we call it, of anxiety.

As an example of how poorly we understand mental health conditions, look at how broad the medications are in the way that they affect the mind. There are ADHD medications that are stimulating, and there are medications that are sedating. Some were designed for use in treating high blood pressure, and some that used to be antidepressants are now rebranded as ADHD medications.

We just don't understand the underlying causes, and when there's more than one treatment for a condition, that means we really don't fully understand that condition. To be clear, the goal isn't to reduce each condition to one treatment option—

rather, it's to understand why a particular treatment is the correct choice for one person and not for another.

Some of the modern advances in psychiatry have tried to alleviate this problem by using artificial intelligence (AI) with large language models (LLMs)[10] to understand patients by looking at how they talk in an intake interview, what words they choose when they fill out questionnaires, and how they interact with staff—all to predict their diagnosis. It's a movement towards a more objective, biomarker-based method of diagnosis, but it leans on subjective diagnostic criteria from the DSM and subjective interpretation of the data. And as I demonstrated earlier, the label doesn't predict treatment response in our current model. Without roots in biological systems, selecting a treatment is still a gamble even with more advanced medicines and therapies.

There is a strong held belief in mental health that a diagnosis holds the key to identifying the correct treatment (like it is in almost all other medical fields). But in psychiatry, potentially due to its subjectivity along with the complexity of the brain and semantics, a diagnosis often doesn't get you close enough to the right treatment.[11]

Even though we're moving in a more objective direction, a better use of LLMs would be to predict the qEEG *phenotype* of a person who would respond to a specific medication or

10 Obradovich, N., Khalsa, S. S., Khan, W. U., et al. (2024). Opportunities and risks of large language models in psychiatry. *NPP: Digital Psychiatry and Neuroscience,* 2, 8.

11 Poirot, M. G. et al. (2024). Treatment response prediction in major depressive disorder using multimodal MRI and clinical data: Secondary analysis of a randomized clinical trial. *American Journal of Psychiatry,181*(3), 223–233.

certain treatment and intervention. We should be using LLMs to predict an effective *intervention* rather than using them solely to make a diagnosis. A LLM built on a flawed foundation will only amplify the issues.

> A **phenotype** is the visible expression of a genetic characteristic combined with environmental factors, whereas the **genotype** is the gene itself. Think of the genotype as the recipe, the phenotype as the finished dish, and the environment like the cook, which can have a huge impact on the way the final dish is presented and tastes.
>
> In psychiatry, we don't routinely look at the genotype, but we can study the phenotype. Measuring brain activity through a qEEG that shows results in high temporal resolution, within milliseconds, offers a window into a person's brain function in nearly real time, providing us with a visible and testable expression of their phenotype.

The Emotional and Financial Toll of Subjectivity

For Patients and Their Family

The consequences of subjectivity can have heartbreaking knock-on effects for patients and their families—not only because of the stigma that can accompany a diagnosis, but also because they may potentially spend years trying to understand and live with a condition that they *may not even have.*

I have witnessed in my two decades of practice that psychiatry has undeniably helped lots of people. But there's so much variability—not only within the potential diagnoses and treatments patients are subjected to, but also within the methods psychiatrists will use. Some providers rely heavily on screening tests for common conditions, while others will schedule four visits with a patient before prescribing anything.

One of the cornerstones of medicine is the *feedback loop*, when the doctor uses routine tests to validate or adjust treatment. So psychiatrists must (yet again) rely on their subjective interpretation of a patient's response to decide whether they're on the right track with treatment.

If you go to a doctor describing that, "I'm struggling with energy, and I'm out of shape, eat poorly, and don't exercise," the doctor will most likely think it's a lifestyle-related condition and run a test. When they do the test, they'll see your triglycerides are high or your blood sugar is abnormal, or find another issue. They'll then give you two medicines and tell you to come back in six weeks when they'll take more blood and look at the lab tests to see if you're moving in the right direction.

In mental health care, they don't do that. Your provider may diagnose you with depression and prescribe an antidepressant, but they're relying on *your subjective interpretation* of your feelings and *their subjective interpretation* of your mood alongside the way you present yourself in the session to decide if the treatment is working or not.

Even if *all* psychiatrists agree that a specific person is depressed, the agreement on treatment is not going to be uniform. Providers tend to have medications that they prefer to prescribe either because they have noticed patients responding better to them in their practice or because they are easily available.

Some providers will recommend a combination of behavioral treatments, while others will exclusively prescribe medication. By working with providers around the world, we are able to observe regional variations to diagnosing and prescribing trends as well.

This itself may lead to the blame game. If the treatment doesn't work, it's not that the diagnosis was off target: perhaps the patient wasn't doing what they needed to do, or they weren't doing the self-care that they needed to prioritize. So when treatments fail, medications pile up, diagnoses shift, and the number of side effects increases, we should be asking, "Was this risk preventable?"

Seemingly logical, there is this idea that the treatment proves the diagnosis. If you give someone stimulants, many people will feel better as dopamine floods their receptors. But does that mean they have ADHD and that they should have special accommodations in school?

On the other hand, if they don't feel good on stimulants, feel anxious and can't sleep, does that mean they have a sleep disorder too? Really, the problem might be that the treatment missed the mark to begin with. If you start with a loose foundation and then you find the treatment isn't working, is it because the diagnosis was wrong? Or is it because you know you've uncovered some other issue as a result?

Further confusing the issue is the fact that feeling better on a drug does not automatically validate the diagnosis. As we discussed, feeling better on stimulants is common and doesn't prove someone has ADHD just like feeling better after a morning coffee doesn't indicate sleep disruption or a caffeine deficiency. And the placebo effect further muddies the waters.

> The **placebo effect** refers to an improvement in the patient's condition after being administered an inactive drug or ineffective treatment, suggesting that the improvement is due to the patient's belief in the treatment.

These issues often lead to patients feeling like failures if they don't respond well to a treatment, even though this isn't their fault. And, for people with mental health concerns, these feelings can be devastating. Eventually, if things don't work out, people get to this place of despair where they think, "I've gone to 12 people; I have 12 different diagnoses. How am I failing? Why is my brain broken?" People can live with a bad hip or shoulder, but if you identify as a person with a broken brain, where's your refuge?

Recently, I conducted a brain scan on a boy who had serious self-injurious behavior almost every other day, cutting or injuring himself. And he has great brain patterns, but his environment just doesn't work for him as an 11-year old in fifth grade. Traditional mental health labels might have the patient thinking, "I'm defective. I'm an aggressive kid. I have oppositional defiant disorder"; whereas the truth is, he's oppositional when backed into a corner because he feels overwhelmed. So I suggested we put him in an individually curated environment where he wouldn't be as overwhelmed and to see if that label would still stick.

The brain wasn't broken—the external environment just didn't fit the brain and its traits.

For Providers

One of the biggest problems facing psychiatric providers today is burnout. The 2023 Medscape survey shows that 30% of male and 46% of female psychiatrists are struggling with burnout, depression, or both.[12] This may be a reflection of the fact that they don't have a lot of clarity on the success of their diagnoses and treatments because of all the subjectivity, which doesn't lend itself to satisfaction with the profession. Psychiatry also has had to defend itself in medicine for a long time. There's been a lot of talk of whether psychiatry is even a branch of medicine at all because it is so different from all the other specialties and sometimes gets stigmatized as a softer pseudoscience.

Providers can also, perhaps without realizing that they're doing it, start to get biased in their treatments and diagnoses simply because there aren't any objective guideposts to help keep them on track. In my experience, doctors gravitate towards certain diagnostic labels. For example, certain doctors diagnose 80% of their patients with ADHD. But, are their patients actually attention deficit, or are the psychiatrists seeing what they want to see? Or are patients who believe they're depressed seeking out a provider that will confirm their diagnoses? It's hard to say without any objective evidence. The same applies to treatments. Providers also use different medicines in different clinics. There are some medicines that certain providers won't touch while others will use that same medicine constantly.

12 Medscape Psychiatry Burnout & Depression Report. (2023).

I believe this comes down to what's called reification, when the provider tries to turn something subjective into something objective. But the biggest problem with this approach is that it can create tunnel vision from the provider that bases their treatment schedule on subjective criteria to the patient who now sees themselves through a certain mental health lens. And all of this leads to self-fulfilling prophecies, when patients will start to behave in certain ways due to their beliefs that this is how they're supposed to act—all the while confirming their psychiatrist's diagnosis.

Subjectivity in psychiatry essentially means that most people involved are guessing, but there's a veneer of respectability and science that stops people from realizing how deep the problem goes.

I once worked with a young child who was completely nonverbal and very aggressive, lashing out at people, especially his mother, multiple times per day. He had received multiple diagnoses and his caregivers were considering putting him on antipsychotic medication.

We noticed some physical issues that weren't being addressed, so we decided to run a panel of gut and metabolic markers—which showed significant abnormalities. We started treatment to address these underlying biological issues and his aggression dramatically decreased almost completely. His episodes decreased in intensity and frequency, and he became more responsive. All of this without having to resort to further medication.

This wasn't a behavioral problem; this wasn't autism or oppositional defiant disorder. Instead, it was a physiological problem manifesting as a psychiatric one, and this situation is more common than you may think.

In the next chapter we're going to look closely at one of the main cornerstones and potential root causes of this subjectivity—the DSM, also known as the "bible of psychiatry"—and how it has contributed to the stagnation of the field in terms of diagnosis and treatment.

Summary

- Psychiatry is one of the only fields of medicine left that relies almost entirely on subjective testing. While there is a thin veneer of objectivity, the truth is that most psychiatrists are making educated guesses to arrive at diagnoses, and then make even more educated guesses to determine the treatments.
- People with mental health concerns may bounce from one diagnosis and treatment to another, all at great financial and emotional cost.
- A diagnosis is not a predictor of treatment outcome, further extending the time between identifying the problem and coming up with an effective solution.
- Subjectivity also affects providers. They have to defend their field against accusations of it being pseudoscience and, at times, have to watch their patients struggle as they try various treatments when not successful.

Chapter 2

The Flat Earth of Psychiatry

Sophie's Story

Every professional Sophie saw had a version of the same approach: asking Sophie questions about her feelings, her situation and whether her parents or family had a history of mental illness. Every appointment followed the same pattern, and Mark started feeling like he was watching every specialist run right into the same brick wall.

After one particularly extensive evaluation session, Dr. Watson, Sophie's latest psychiatrist noted "Sophie's struggling a lot with focus and organization, and it seems to intensify when she needs to perform. It's like stress triggers some kind of shutdown response."

"Yes, that's true," Mark said, "But it doesn't explain how she can hyperfocus on specific projects but collapse on routine tasks."

"And it doesn't explain why she also anticipates failure before it happens," Linda, Mark's wife, chimed in. "Yesterday, she had a complete meltdown about a math test that she hadn't started studying for; yet, she was already convinced that she'd fail even though it's work she's previously been comfortable with."

After some pondering, Dr. Watson said, "While Sophie meets the criteria for ADHD inattentive type, I think there are some complicating factors that warrant a broader approach. She may have ADHD with comorbid anxiety disorder, likely with some emotional dysregulation that could indicate early bipolar tendencies."

Mark started at the psychiatrist in disbelief. "So now she's got three conditions?"

"Based on the DSM and my experience, yes." Dr. Watson didn't even blink as she confirmed her new diagnosis.

"Now, I'm not a mental health professional," Linda was getting visibly agitated, mirroring Mark's feelings, "But when a doctor doesn't know what's going on, they usually run tests, right? Blood work, scans, that type of thing. Why aren't you doing anything like that? All I've seen you do is ask some questions, fill in some forms, and complete some checklists. Why is that?"

"I understand your frustration, but all of my diagnoses are based on careful clinical assessment." Dr. Watson patted Linda's hand reassuringly, "Trust me, we all want what's best for Sophie."

Privately, Mark had started to wonder if a careful clinical assessment was enough. Sophie had seen several providers at this point and each one was as confident in their diagnosis as Dr. Watson was to no avail. Sophie wasn't getting better, and Mark couldn't see a light at the end of the tunnel. How could he be confident that Dr. Watson's solution was the right one? All of her decisions were based on the DSM—as were those of her predecessors. Was this reliance the fatal flaw, the common mistake that all these providers were doomed to repeat?

As a licensed clinical social worker with 15 years of experience, Mark understood the mental health system better than most parents. He'd guided countless families through similar challenges and had always felt confident in his ability to navigate complex cases. But Sophie's situation was exposing limitations in the system that his professional experience had helped him overlook.

"I know all these providers are skilled," Mark told Linda during one of their late-night conversations. "I've referred patients to Dr. Watson myself, and she's helped many teenagers. But watching Sophie get more confused and withdrawn despite everyone's best efforts is making me question everything I thought I knew about treatment."

Mark found himself caught between his professional understanding and his parental desperation. He knew that therapy and medication could be effective, but he was watching his daughter disappear despite receiving treatment from some of the best providers in their area.

The Origin and History of the DSM

Every mental health provider in the United States is intimately familiar with the DSM. It forms the core of most mental health curricula, and its language, particularly around diagnostic labels, has entered into the common lexicon. People will often refer to themselves as "anxious", "depressed", even "bipolar" or "manic"—all terms that were popularized and normalized in the DSM.

The fifth iteration of the DSM (DSM-5) is widely considered to be the gold standard of psychiatric diagnosis. It aims to be a comprehensive list of mental health disorders and their symptoms and to assist psychiatrists in arriving at a diagnosis by comparing a patient's experience and symptoms to the book's description of a condition. The DSM has changed dramatically since its first publication in 1952, both in its view of psychiatric disorders and the number of conditions it describes.

The History of the DSM

People have a tendency to think in categories. It's almost instinctual to create labels for things because they create the illusion of clarity and order.

The same holds true for medical professionals. Most early efforts to gather information about mental illness in the United States were actually driven by the U.S. Bureau of the Census to get more comprehensive data about the country's population. But by the end of the Second World War, the landscape had shifted and both the military and health care professionals had identified the need for a comprehensive classification system.

The first iteration of the DSM (DSM-I), published in 1952, was based on the World Health Organization's International Classification of Diseases (ICD). The fundamental assumption of the DSM-I was that mental health concerns were responses to biological, social, and psychological stimuli and could vary dramatically in severity. This assumption reinforced the view that mental health conditions were not permanent illnesses of the brain, but were more likely to be responses to the environment along with certain character traits and the social context of the time.

Initially, this iteration of the DSM didn't make much of an impact on the psychiatric community as a diagnostic tool. Its main impact, rather, was setting the stage for standardized categories of mental disorders. The second iteration of the DSM (DSM-II) continued this trend of focusing on categorizing and describing mental disorders without offering much advice about diagnosis.

The third iteration of the DSM (DSM-III), published in 1980, marked a turning point for the book, cementing its place as the so-called bible of psychiatric diagnosis. The DSM-III expanded the number of mental disorder categories from 182 in the DSM-II to 265. Some of these expansions were subdivisions of existing categories, while others were completely new disorders.

But what really cemented the DSM-III's place in psychiatry is that it included advice on how to diagnose conditions instead of just cataloging them; it even included standards for differential diagnosis when conditions shared symptoms. The DSM-III also marked a shift from viewing mental health disorders as a response to biological, social, and psychological stimuli to viewing them as illnesses of the brain instead.

This is the point where psychiatry became more rigid, shifting from a fluid understanding of mental health conditions as responses of the brain to having a fixed diagnostic identity.

Differential diagnosis is the method of distinguishing between two conditions that share similar symptoms. Fatigue is a common symptom of many conditions like anemia or a vitamin B deficiency and isn't enough on its own to help a doctor make a diagnosis. Instead, the doctor will run additional tests to confirm or rule out a specific condition.

In psychiatry, a differential diagnosis is made without objective testing and relies on more interviews and checklists than physical scientific evidence.

From this point on, the DSM (and its assumptions about psychiatric conditions) has pervaded psychiatric medicine. Students are expected to test patients according to criteria from the latest version, psychiatric textbooks are structured according to the disorders listed in the DSM, and even academics are instructed to use terms and definitions found in the DSM.

Almost every piece of work produced by the mental health field in the last 50 years has in some way been influenced by the language and underlying assumptions found in the DSM.

The fourth and fifth iterations of the DSM refine the diagnostic framework set by the DSM-III, but they don't really do much to challenge its fundamental assumption: mental health conditions are identifiable *diseases* rather than fluid responses to biological, environmental, and social stresses described in the original DSM-I.

At this point, hundreds, if not thousands, of psychiatric experts, providers, and academics are involved in developing the DSM. The latest revision of the DSM-5 was the work of 200 experts who took approximately two-and-a-half years to review current psychiatric literature and identify where the DSM was outdated. The text was also examined by a working group that focused on identifying potential issues with discrimination, racism, and stigmatizing language.

However, even as the language in the DSM becomes more modern, the framework remains the same: outdated with rigid categories, little biological insight, and few tools to predict what treatments will actually work.

How Psychiatrists Use the DSM

The DSM permeates psychiatric training. Textbooks have chapters based on DSM categories, academic literature refers to DSM conditions, and the checklists that psychiatrists use are based largely on DSM criteria.

The most recent version of the DSM, the DSM-5-TR, has three major sections: the introduction that outlines how professionals should use the book, the diagnostic criteria that makes up the bulk of the book, and a section about specific assessment tools and checklists.

Each condition in the current DSM has several crucial pieces of information:

- The diagnostic classification and code.
- A set of criteria that a patient must meet to obtain a diagnosis. This includes a set of symptoms, the required length and persistence of these symptoms that could describe the severity of the disorder, and other disorders with the same symptoms (to help with the differential diagnosis).
- A comprehensive description of the disorder that includes potential diagnostic issues and the consequences of the condition along with its prevalence.

Mental health providers can also use various checklists to give a patient's symptoms a numerical value. These checklists are almost always based on the diagnostic criteria in the DSM and create a way for providers to quantify the severity of a disorder. But while these checklists feel scientific, they are based on assumptions that we will discuss further in the chapter.

How the DSM Has Stalled Psychiatry's Progress into the Modern Age

A Veneer of Objectivity

The DSM has much influence on how mental health professionals approach and view mental disorders. Because the DSM categorizes these disorders by symptoms and uses high-level psychiatric language, it can appear objective, and psychiatrists using the DSM will feel that they are arriving at an objective diagnosis. Effectively, I would argue that the DSM gives the *illusion* of precision without actually providing an objective foundation.

Psychiatrists are often trained using the DSM. Some textbooks even organize their content according to categories in the DSM. This means that the book is deeply entrenched in psychiatry, and few psychiatrists ever consider questioning its usefulness or accuracy.

Let's look at a concrete example of how the DSM can fool providers. The patient will often fill in a questionnaire or checklist like the Patient Health Questionnaire (PHQ-9) or the Generalized Anxiety Disorder (GAD-7), which are used to assess patients with depression or anxiety, respectively. These checklists are based on DSM criteria and provide a way to decide the severity of a patient's condition.

But what many providers don't realize is there is little actual scientific reasoning for why a GAD-7 score between 10-14 is moderate anxiety, whereas one ranging between 15–21 is severe anxiety. The cutoff point, despite influencing how the patient may approach treatment and even their view of their condition, is almost completely arbitrary.

So even if the provider worked with the patient to fill out the questionnaire accurately and objectively, there's no way to eliminate subjectivity because it's been built into the questionnaire. The authors of these checklists used the DSM to develop their criteria, and then inserted their own arbitrary cutoff points based on the subjective experiences in their practice.

This lack of objectivity in the checklists is confirmed by the fact that only 50% of patients diagnosed with major depression using the PHQ-9 actually had major depression.[13]

As another example, let's look at a hypothetical patient's scores on two standardized instruments that are commonly used in psychiatric practice.

Conners' ADHD Rating Scale Results:

- Inattention: T-score 73 (significantly elevated)
- Hyperactivity/Impulsivity: T-score 58 (average range)
- Overall ADHD Index: T-score 67 (elevated)

Beck Youth Inventories Results:

- Depression: T-score 68 (moderately elevated)
- Anxiety: T-score 74 (significantly elevated)
- Anger: T-score 62 (mildly elevated)

Most providers will see these scores and see an objective measure of the patient's inattention, hyperactivity, depression, anxiety, and anger levels. But the reasoning behind why a T-score of 73 represents significantly elevated ADHD symptoms while 67 indicates elevated overall functioning is based on statistical modeling rather than biological validation. While not completely arbitrary, these cutoff points that influence treatment are rooted in subjectivity, in assumptions, and modeling rather than what's happening in the brain.

13 Levis, B., Benedetti, A., & Thombs, B. D. (2019). Accuracy of Patient Health Questionnaire-9 (PHQ-9) for screening to detect major depression: Individual participant data meta-analysis. *British Medical Journal*, 365.

Psychiatry has been inherently subjective from the very beginning, as it was impossible to study the brain directly, and the practice relied on people's reporting and psychiatrist's intuition and experience. Instead of using objective biological data, the DSM formalized these subjective markers as objective fact. And this then feeds into the tools used by psychiatrists and the language they use, further entrenching subjectivity into the very fabric of psychiatry.

Impeding Diagnostic Reliability

It's generally assumed within medicine that if providers are presented with the same set of symptoms and test data they will arrive at the same diagnosis and same treatment plan. There will always be some variation, of course; some providers prefer a more aggressive treatment option while others may be able to detect nuances within test results to arrive at a more accurate diagnosis. But in general, diagnostic reliability is one of the cornerstones of modern medicine.

Except in psychiatry. During the DSM-5's development, several trials were conducted to assess its reliability as a diagnostic tool, and the results were concerning. A large focus on the DSM-5 was to assist providers with differential diagnoses, particularly in confounding conditions such as schizophrenia, bipolar disorder, and schizoaffective disorder, where there are many similarities in symptoms and presentation. While the reliability of diagnosis between these three conditions was improved, the study also highlighted the deeply concerning lack of reliability in major depressive disorder, obsessive compulsive disorder (OCD)-type disorders, and antisocial personality disorders.[14]

This lack of reliability isn't due to provider inadequacy; it is because the DSM remains a tool that relies on subjective symptoms to identify categories instead of trying to decipher the root biological cause of these symptoms.

The DSM vs. Biological Testing

The DSM is psychiatry trying to make sense of something through a lens of limited information. Have you ever made a judgment about something with information that is missing? Of course, we all have, and then we realize our mistakes afterward when we get more relevant data. And that's what psychiatry has done for decades: made judgments about people and put them in certain categories without all of the much-needed biological information.

In the past, there was no way to look at the brain, and even if we were to cut open someone's head, it wouldn't tell you anything about what was going on in their mind. Even if you physically poked around, it still wouldn't tell you anything (and doing so would be extremely unethical). We couldn't see consciousness or complex thought, so we had to be led by subjectivity. There was no other way.

Psychiatry was doing the best it could with a limited set of tools, and despite the shortcomings of the DSM, psychiatry has helped millions of people across the world. But now, imagine

---

14 Freedman, R., Lewis, D. A., Michels, R., Pine, D. S., Schultz, S. K., Tamminga, C. A., Gabbard, G. O., Gau, S. S. F., Javitt, D. C., Oquendo, M. A. & Shrout, P. E. (2013). The initial field trials of DSM-5: New blooms and old thorns. *American Journal of Psychiatry, 170*(1), 1–5.

a world where we can look at your brain objectively through a whole new lens based on information that we didn't even know existed. That's where biologically grounded testing comes in.

Of course, psychiatrists have been burned by biological theories before. The commonly accepted theory that chemical imbalances in the brain cause mental health issues (neurotransmitter theory) has come under close scrutiny in recent years.

Neurotransmitter theory arose in the 1950s, when scientists noticed that certain medications intended for other conditions had mood altering effects. For example, tuberculosis drugs were found to elevate mood, sometimes even causing manic or psychotic symptoms.[15] Research into schizophrenia in the '60s identified a link between dopamine pathways and the condition. This same research also found that antipsychotic medications targeting dopamine receptors helped alleviate these symptoms.[16]

> A **neurotransmitter** is a chemical that transmits a signal from a nerve cell to either another nerve cell or a muscle or gland. Neurotransmitters control functions like your heart beating, muscle movements, hormone production, hunger and thirst, and also mood, memory, and thoughts.

Despite the initial enthusiasm, neurotransmitter theory faced challenges; not all patients responded to the same treatment,

15 Samouco, A. I. C. B & Alves, S. P. (2023), Isoniazid-induced mania and the history of antidepressant drugs: Case report and literature review. *Bipolar Disorders*, 25, 84–87.

16 Stępnicki P., Kondej M., & Kaczor A. A. (2018) Current concepts and treatments of schizophrenia. *Molecules*, (8), 2087.

and a landmark study showed that patients diagnosed with depression did not all respond to SSRIs (which would be the case if the neurotransmitter theory was true).[17]

> A **selective serotonin reuptake inhibitor** (SSRI) is a drug that blocks the reuptake, or recycling, of serotonin and increases its levels in the brain. Many common antidepressants are SSRIs, including Zoloft™, Prozac™, and Celexa™.

While neurotransmitters provide a foundation for developing psychiatric medication, they don't provide the whole picture. No single neurotransmitter can explain the complexity of human behavior. Today, mental health disorders are understood to be a result from a complex interplay of genetics, environmental factors, and neurobiological factors that may involve a neurotransmitter imbalance.

Unfortunately, this growing criticism of neurotransmitter theory makes many psychiatrists wary about looking at other biological tests and causes of mental health.

A very appealing, biologically based test that provides an alternative to the DSM is qEEG, which measures electrical activity in the brain through a series of electrodes placed on the skull. The test is already the go-to diagnostic method for identifying or localizing conditions like epilepsy, brain tumors, and inflammation of the brain. Electroencephalogram (EEG) is already a standard diagnostic tool in neurology; it's time psychiatry caught up.

17 Poirot, M. G. et al. (2024). Treatment response prediction in major depressive disorder using multimodal MRI and clinical data: Secondary analysis of a randomized clinical trial. *American Journal of Psychiatry,181*(3), 223–233.

Quantitative electroencephalography is a more sophisticated variant of a standard EEG that further analyzes the signals obtained through the test and helps providers visualize brain activity and correlate it to various behaviors. We'll look at it in much more detail in Chapter 4.

One of the most common criticisms of qEEG is that its findings don't map neatly onto various DSM-based categories. For example, people diagnosed with depression can have different brain patterns that don't correspond with various DSM depression criteria. Many patients with ADHD-type brain patterns may not display ADHD symptoms, and critics of qEEG will use this to say that qEEG cannot be used to diagnose ADHD.

This category problem extends across psychiatric conditions. Depression, for example, shows remarkably different trends in brain scans. Some patients demonstrate externalization patterns, directing emotional energy outward through irritability or agitation. Others show internalization patterns, turning emotions inward through withdrawal and self-criticism. Still others display cognitive slowing similar to what we see in traumatic brain injury cases.

Most fascinating to me is how often what appears to be depression is actually undiagnosed ADHD profiles, particularly in females. These patients present with classic depression symptoms—low mood, poor concentration, low self-esteem—but their brain scans reveal ADHD-type patterns. This predictably explains why they respond poorly to antidepressants and mood stabilizers but show remarkable improvement with ADHD-targeted interventions.

From a systems neuroscience perspective, the reliance on the DSM over biological testing is looking at the situation backwards. qEEG looks at the root cause of brain activity and mental health conditions, whereas the DSM is a set of subjective criteria and symptoms that tries to describe what's going on in the mind. One of these is based in biology and relies on measurable, quantifiable data; the other is the DSM. We should be considering updating the DSM to reflect biology instead of trying to fit biology into DSM-based criteria.

The DSM Is Holding Psychiatric Medicine Back

If psychiatry continues to operate within the DSM framework, it will struggle to evolve into a data-driven, biological marker-based field like any other specialized field of medicine. The DSM isn't the solution; it's the obstacle.

To be clear, this isn't a critique of clinicians who use the DSM, as they are also deeply affected by the drawbacks of the system. Rather, it's a critique of the system that limits them.

I like to compare the DSM to the flat Earth theory of centuries ago. As humanity, we didn't know that anything else existed because every time one of us tried to go to the perceived edge of the world, we fell off a cliff. For psychiatry, this has happened with neurotransmitters, and now there's a reluctance to try again. A psychiatrist friend of mine said that psychiatrists are so gun shy about genetic tests or any biologically based testing because they've been told for years, "We're going to have a test that will help you." And in the past, none of them worked.

For the last 30 years, people have been trying to promote qEEG. What happens is that someone will say, "A high theta/beta ratio is consistent or predictive of an ADHD diagnosis." But when they test a hundred children diagnosed with ADHD and measure their theta/beta ratio, only half of them have high theta/beta ratios.[18] And it's tempting to think, "This test is inaccurate, it doesn't work." But the actual problem is that ADHD isn't a single diagnosis; it's a highly heterogeneous mix of symptoms that the DSM has decided falls under one umbrella. The qEEG shows the reality of the situation: that much more than *one brain pattern* can cause the cluster of symptoms known as ADHD, thus explaining the various treatment responses we see clinically.

This wasn't a failed test but rather a misaligned framework where the categories have no basis in biology, and the qEEG (a biological test) highlights that.

We are currently in a situation where we have a usable and functional tool that has the potential to transform the field. And yet, the old paradigm remains surprisingly persistent despite the fact that the DSM is not rooted in biology.

And this is holding modern advances in psychiatry back just like the Church held the round Earth theory back for decades and stifled exploration and scientific inquiry. The shift away from the flat earth theory of the DSM is coming, but I have to wonder how many patients and providers will suffer before that shift towards evidence-based objective testing happens.

18 Picken, C., Clarke, A. R., Barry, R. J., McCarthy, R., & Selikowitz, M. (2020). The theta/beta ratio as an index of cognitive processing in adults with the combined type of attention deficit hyperactivity disorder. *Clinical EEG Neuroscience*, *51*(3),167–173.

In addition to holding back diagnosis, the DSM holds back treatment research because we can't really expect innovation from a model that doesn't reflect biology. The neurotransmitter theory resulted in a whole host of pharmaceutical interventions from antipsychotics to SSRIs. No doubt these drugs have helped billions of people.

By focusing on biology we can allow researchers the freedom to understand the underlying physical and biological causes of these conditions without having to worry about the subjective (arguably meaningless) diagnosis. Moving away from the DSM could promote innovative treatments and increased precision in the field, helping even more people get the assistance they need.

The DSM and the Healthcare Industry

The DSM provides the framework for categorizing symptoms and assisting providers with obtaining a diagnosis. It also forms the basis of the billing codes used by insurance companies when determining whether to reimburse a patient for their condition, which in turn, ultimately forces providers to use the DSM when practicing their craft.

The result is a system optimized for administrative efficiency rather than biological understanding—like a sorting machine designed to process claims quickly rather than help people heal.

Neither system reveals what's actually happening in the brain or addresses the tremendous diversity within diagnostic categories. Here's what makes this particularly troubling:

two patients with identical DSM diagnoses and matching billing codes may not share *any* symptoms, yet they receive the *same* treatment protocols because the system manipulates providers into categorical thinking rather than individualized understanding.

This deep symbiotic relationship between the DSM and the health care insurance and pharmaceutical industries further entrenches the DSM into psychiatry despite growing criticism of its effectiveness as a diagnostic tool.

When new DSM editions are published, pharmaceutical companies quickly align their drug marketing to fit the newly defined disorders. For example, premenstrual dysphoric disorder was officially recognized in 1994. Around the same time, Prozac™ was repackaged as Seraphim™ and specifically marketed to treat premenstrual dysphoric disorder. The only difference between Prozac™ and Seraphim was the branding and the color of the pill.

In the US, drug companies can also use the DSM and its categorization of mental conditions to encourage people to self-diagnose: Zoloft™ commercials promoted the idea that depression is a serotonin deficiency, leading millions of people to ask their health care providers for the drug based on nothing more than an ad and a self-diagnosis.

Insurance companies also benefit from the current entrenchment of the DSM. These companies rely on DSM-based diagnosis codes. If a condition isn't found in the DSM, the insurance won't cover its treatment. For instance, Pediatric Autoimmune Neuropsychiatric Disorders Associated with

Streptococcal Infections (PANDAS) manifests as a mental health condition (tics and obsessive compulsive disorder) but is rooted in the aftermath of a strep infection. And since there isn't a diagnostic code, many insurance companies won't cover immune-based treatments for what they perceive to be a mental health condition.

Clinicians often find themselves in an uncomfortable position of having to fit a patient into a DSM category, even if they may suspect a patient doesn't really fit into that category. This encourages mislabeling, which can have severe and lasting consequences for the patient (who now believes they have a condition they may not actually have), simply to get that patient treatment they don't have to pay for out of pocket.

This can also contribute to overdiagnosis as many clinicians will label patients with a disorder to justify pharmacological treatment, which can often be extremely expensive if not covered by insurance. This inflates the number of people diagnosed with psychiatric conditions, reinforcing the DSM's dominance in spite of its lack of efficiency.

To recap, let's take a collective look at this information. The pharmaceutical companies develop and market drugs aligned with the DSM-defined conditions. Direct-to-consumer advertising encourages more people to seek treatment. Insurance companies only reimburse providers for DSM-recognized conditions. So the clinicians, then, must diagnose based on the DSM criteria even though they don't entirely fit into the subjective categories, and the DSM expands with new disorders, creating new drug markets and insurance codes. Meanwhile, psychiatry remains stuck in this cycle, prioritizing symptom-based treatment over true neuroscience-based diagnoses.

To put things bluntly, the DSM serves the industry, not the patients. It doesn't exist because it's the best way to diagnose mental illness or support providers; it exists because it maintains a system for pharmaceutical and insurance companies. The DSM enforces symptom-based diagnoses, preventing the integration of biological objective testing, and insurance companies enforce the DSM's authority, ensuring that only DSM-defined conditions are billable.

So are we diagnosing mental health conditions based on what's best for the patient or based on what's best for the highest rates of profitability in the industry?

The Consequences of Relying Solely on the DSM for Diagnosis and Treatment

The biggest problem with the DSM is its inconsistency due to its subjectivity. If the DSM was truly objective, the same patient would always get the same diagnosis. But that doesn't happen, because the DSM isn't rooted in biology. The way the DSM was formulated relies on the subjective interpretation of subjective symptoms, while even the tests based on the DSM don't provide reliable results.

The most common condition plaguing the US is hypertension. If you go to a hundred doctors and they all have blood pressure cuffs that are properly calibrated and work correctly, you will get a hypertension diagnosis from every single one of them. If you have depression and you go to a hundred psychiatrists, you will, very likely, get more diagnoses than depression.

Even more importantly, a DSM diagnosis is not a *predictor of treatment success.*[19] Not every person with ADHD responds to the same medication, and patients can spend years trialing various drugs with different side effects before possibly finding the solution that works for them.

For example, stimulants, which, in part, increase dopamine, are commonly prescribed for ADHD. Yet, not all individuals with ADHD respond well to them. If ADHD was purely a dopamine issue, the response to stimulants should be universal—you would just give people more dopamine, and they would feel better. But this isn't the case, and another common medication for ADHD, atomoxetine, targets a completely different neurotransmitter entirely.

All of this leads to the types of consequences we described in Chapter 1, which we will cover in even more detail in Chapter 3.

Bipolar disorder is a difficult condition to diagnose and treat. When I was in clinical practice, we often had patients coming to the qEEG clinic when their bipolar treatment failed (which is a lot more often than you'd think), and what we often saw was a combination of ADHD and variants of autism in their brain scans. If you put those two together—the social disconnect of

19 Poirot, M. G. et al. (2024). Treatment response prediction in major depressive disorder using multimodal MRI and clinical data: Secondary analysis of a randomized clinical trial. *American Journal of Psychiatry,181*(3), 223–233.

autism with the impulsivity that accompanies ADHD—those symptoms could fit the DSM criteria for bipolar disorder.

And unlike depression or ADHD, where the stigma is mostly removed, a bipolar diagnosis comes with consequences like repeated blood screenings for medical levels. Plus, it stays on your record, which can affect job screenings and government or military work. Getting that diagnosis wrong has huge implications for the patient.

Moving Away from the DSM

Criticism against the DSM is growing.[20,21] Providers are noticing that using the DSM and relying on subjective interpretations of symptoms can lead to a host of problems, including misdiagnosing patients based on cultural differences, biases in diagnoses (providers tending towards one or two types of diagnosis), and biases in treatment.

In academic circles, the shift away from the DSM began over a decade ago. The National Institute of Mental Health (NIMH) announced in 2013 that it would move away from funding research based on DSM categories, instead relying on a set of Research Domain Criteria that incorporates behavioral and biological evidence. Unfortunately, this shift did not focus on the DSM as a diagnostic tool, which the NIMH still called the gold standard of diagnosis, but instead opened up research beyond the constraints of the DSM.

20 Craddock, N., Mynors-Wallis, L. (2014). Psychiatric diagnosis: Impersonal, imperfect and important. *British Journal of Psychiatry*, *204*(2), 93–95.

21 Glannon, W. (2022). Biomarkers in psychiatric disorders. *Cambridge Quarterly of Healthcare Ethics*, *31*(4), 444–452.

Another hint that psychiatry is moving away from the DSM comes from psychedelic research. Psychiatrists are focusing increasingly on neuroscience and how psychedelics affect the brain itself, showing a shift in thinking away from symptom-based treatments and towards biological underpinnings.

Currently, psychedelics are shaping and creating conversations around the dysfunction within psychiatry and are showing patients that they can get help independent of their diagnosis. But we have to be careful to not get thrown right back in the same model where these medicines are used based on a diagnostic label. Because if we do, we're going to end up in the same boat: applying psychedelics to treat a DSM-based label that may or may not work.

> "Psychedelics represent a major breakthrough in psychiatric care, not only for their effectiveness but also for challenging the long-standing, reductionist model focused on symptom suppression. This approach introduces a paradigm shift, one that actually revives an ancient perspective on medicine that has been used in traditional medicine cultures around the world for millennia. This approach integrates therapy, harnesses expectation effects, and leverages the mind-body connection and neuroplasticity to drive profound psychological transformation. Rather than targeting isolated symptoms, it acknowledges that symptoms are part of a larger system, and when that system is in balance, they naturally diminish or become more manageable."
> –Dr. I.A. Malidelis, MD[22]

22 Dr. I.A. Malidelis, MD (Personal communication, March 17, 2025)

The DSM and the AI Revolution

AI in psychiatry is currently a hot topic, especially relating to mental health diagnoses. A recent study looked at how well LLMs can assess psychiatric functioning from patient interviews and clinical descriptions and showed that they could support diagnosing mental health issues.[23]

> A **large language model** (LLM) is a type of advanced AI algorithm that analyzes and responds to human text. For example, ChatGPT is a LLM that can answer questions and even have a realistic-looking dialogue with a human being. LLMs can also evaluate text for certain features, making them useful in psychiatry.

AI can certainly be a huge benefit to the field as long as we understand its *limitations*. AI could be key in biomarker-driven tests, such as qEEG, which often produce huge amounts of data that no human could ever process. AI could also be used as a tool to help us understand the data and make connections on intangible things that no human being can see with their naked eye.

With our partner clinics, we've run tens of thousands of qEEG scans, and AI can help us find patterns faster and easier than we would solely with human understanding. A huge potential benefit is that it can relate these analyses to treatment responsiveness, helping us understand the question: **How**

23 Omar, M., Soffer, S., Charney, A. W., Landi, I., Nadkarni, G. N., & Klang, E. (2024). Applications of large language models in psychiatry: a systematic review. *Frontiers in Psychiatry*, 15, 1422807.

well do people with this type of brain pattern react to these types of treatments? Do they need medication, or can other interventions be enough? That's where I see AI is going to revolutionize psychiatry.

AI could become an extremely useful tool in *predicting* what treatment a patient will respond to based on the information from thousands of other people who have responded to similar treatments. If we train AI properly on objective data, it can become a powerful tool in psychiatry.

Despite the appeal of AI, we also need to understand its potential pitfalls. And I think a lot of that is related to the DSM. If we continue to use the DSM as the framework for LLMs, for example, we'll still be getting results based on a murky foundation. If we're training a model to replicate our broken system, it will do a fantastic job of doing that, and it will confirm the biases that we already have. We have to get away from this way of thinking.

An AI model based on a DSM foundation will continue to perpetuate this broken model under the guise of science, progress, and objectivity, and it's going to look like we're advancing psychiatry. But progress will not be made when that is happening; it's just reinforcing and perpetuating labels on people even more. It will not get us to the underlying biological cause of these mental health concerns. Instead, using this kind of AI model runs the risk of becoming another veneer.

What needs to happen, instead, is that AI should be integrated into *biomarker-driven* science. When you do that, it could help psychiatrists by assisting with their cognitive load for accuracy, and provide meaningful connections based on objective data.

The current qEEG analysis we run has about a dozen values associated with it (even though it can produce significantly more), which we use to derive our metrics. We don't currently need more biomarkers to provide people with treatment options tailored to their brain patterns. Instead, we need providers who adopt the biomarkers that we already have to integrate those into their practices so that they can better understand the nuances of their patients through the lens of strengths and challenges. This will allow providers to create the supportive environment needed to support their patients both internally (biological systems) and externally (environmental systems).

In the last two chapters, we've shown the foundational problems that plague psychiatry. In the next chapter, I'll show how these problems affect patients and their families, providers, and even society at large.

Summary

- The DSM was originally an attempt to categorize various mental health disorders.
- During its development, the DSM became a tool for diagnosing instead of just describing mental health disorders.
- The conditions described in the DSM aren't based on biological information, but instead on subjective reports and symptoms.

- The prominence of the DSM has led to the illusion of precision and has held back more objective tests.
- There is a strong symbiotic relationship between the DSM and insurance and pharmaceutical industries.
- This relationship actively ensures the DSM remains the gold standard of psychiatric diagnosis.
- Blindly accepting the DSM has led psychiatrists to a guessing game where a diagnosis isn't even a reliable predictor of treatment outcome.
- Academics and mental health providers are starting to criticize the DSM and opting for more objective testing.
- AI won't make the DSM more objective and will amplify its issues instead.
- The foundation of psychiatry *must* move towards biological testing that is not simply based on guessing disguised as science.

Chapter 3

The Cost of Guessing

Sophie's Story

Since her initial diagnosis, Sophie has been collecting labels like scout badges. She had been diagnosed with ADHD, generalized anxiety disorder, major depressive disorder, and adjustment disorder with mixed anxiety and depressed mood. Not only did each diagnosis add to her feeling of isolation and shame, but they also failed to help her get better. While the cocktail of medication she was on had stabilized her mood, she still felt despondent, hopeless, and concerned about her future.

Mark was deeply concerned about his daughter's well-being. However, he was also worried about their finances. Despite the fact that he and Linda were full-time professionals in well-paying jobs, Sophie's treatments had started racking up, as did the ongoing visits to specialized clinicians.

Their health insurance had started refusing additional treatments, meaning that every new therapist, medication, or intervention was out of pocket. While her parents told Sophie that "money was no object" if it meant she got better, Sophie was unconvinced that the thousands of dollars they were spending regularly had any effect at all. Mark was also getting worried about the additional strain incorrect treatments were having on them financially and the fact that this put extra pressure on Sophie to get better.

Worse than the financial toll was the emotional and social cost. Sophie had lost most of her friends and struggled to make new ones. She was awkward and angry around her peers, which eventually contributed to decreased school performance. When Sophie was younger, she'd dreamt of becoming a veterinarian and working with animals. Now that dream seemed impossible due to Sophie's poor marks and lack of academic involvement.

"Everyone thinks I'm anxious or lazy," Sophie had written in her journal, which Linda discovered during one of her increasingly frequent checks on her daughter's well-being. "But I'm not. I'm just...gone when I try. Like there's nothing inside when I need to think or feel or be myself."

Sophie's family was also bearing the burden of the guessing game. The financial cost was taking a drastic toll on Linda and Mark's marriage, and they edged closer and closer toward divorce. The only reason they hadn't was due to their concern for Sophie, but their resentment towards each other was growing.

The fact that they couldn't fix their daughter's pain made Mark withdraw into his woodworking while Linda became obsessive and paranoid, constantly vigilant for new developments in her daughter's mental health.

Mark had taken out a second mortgage on the house simply to keep up with paying for the medication and therapist visits, but he hid this from his family to protect them from extra stress. His own practice was suffering as he became increasingly disillusioned with his profession. He started wondering how many of his patients were going through the same thing and how he could have missed it for so many years.

He knew that the situation had reached its breaking point when Linda found a note that Sophie had written and then hidden under her mattress: "Maybe if I wasn't here, everyone could stop trying to figure out what's wrong with me. They could stop spending all this money and energy on someone who's already gone. Their lives would be so much better without me, and they've already lost me so they wouldn't even have to grieve."

While this may sound extreme, this is what hundreds, if not thousands, of American families are facing due to a defective model of diagnosis and treatment. And in this chapter, we'll look at the real-world consequences of psychiatry's guessing game.

The Financial Toll

Before we dive into the individual cost that patients and families need to pay to access health care, let's take a broader look at the economic consequences of the current mental health crisis in the US.

According to a recent working paper for the National Bureau of Economic Research,[24] mental illness costs the US

24 Abramson, B., Boerma, J., & Tsyvinski, A. (2024). Macroeconomics of mental health. *National Bureau of Economic Research*, 32354.

economy $282 billion every year, which is more than what the government spends annually on veteran's benefits and services as well as education combined.[25] This estimate includes factors such as the cost of mental health treatments, lost income, and other less obvious costs like the fact that people with mental health concerns choose lower-paying, less stressful jobs and spend and invest less.

Direct costs

The most devastating financial reality families face isn't the cost of effective treatment; it's the multiplication effect that occurs when initial treatments fail. This creates a cascading series of expenses:

- Additional medications to address side effects or persistent symptoms
- Consultations with multiple specialists seeking different perspectives
- More expensive interventions as first-line treatments fail
- Extended treatment timelines that compound all other costs
- Crisis interventions when symptoms worsen despite treatment

A recent survey of 1,000 Americans revealed that nearly 60% have accumulated over $1,000 in debt to pay for mental health treatments, while 31% consider mental health care financially out of reach.[26] These numbers reflect families trapped in a

25 More information about government spending can be found here: https://fiscaldata.treasury.gov/americas-finance-guide/federal-spending/

26 Abramson, B., Boerma, J., & Tsyvinski, A. 2024. Macroeconomics of Mental Health. *National Bureau of Economic Research*, 32354.

system that forces providers to guess rather than know, making expensive trial and error approaches unavoidable.

The direct costs of mental health treatment multiply dramatically when providers are trapped in subjective diagnostic frameworks. Here's an example of how a potential patient's costs may start racking up due to the multiplicative effects of a failed diagnosis.

Year One Costs:

- Initial psychiatric evaluation: $500
- Monthly therapy sessions: $400/month = $4,800
- Initial medication (sertraline): $30/month = $360
- Follow-up psychiatric visits: $300 quarterly = $1,200
- **Total Year One: $6,860**

Year Two Costs:

- Additional specialist consultations: $1,500
- Multiple medication trials: $200/month = $2,400
- Increased therapy frequency: $600/month = $7,200
- Crisis intervention sessions: $800
- Educational testing and accommodations: $1,200
- **Total Year Two: $13,100**

Year Three Projected Costs:

- Intensive outpatient program: $3,000/month = $36,000
- Multiple medications: $800/month = $9,600
- Ongoing specialist care: $2,400
- Family therapy: $150/week = $7,800
- **Projected Year Three: $55,800**

These escalating costs reflect the diagnostic trap's impact: as providers struggle within subjective frameworks, expenses multiply while outcomes remain poor, potentially causing patients to feel hopeless.

Indirect costs

The direct costs of mental health treatments don't tell the whole story though. Indirect costs refer to secondary ways in which people lose money due to their mental health struggles. These can be things like losing income due to getting fired from work for poor performance, not getting work due to depression, and even lost income from not being able to complete college or high school.

A woman in her 40s came to one of our clinics presenting with chronic fatigue, brain fog, and mood swings. She had been diagnosed with bipolar disorder and was on a cocktail of mood stabilizers and antipsychotics. Unfortunately, these drugs progressively led to worsening fatigue and cognitive decline, and eventually, she lost her job. Due to these effects and her bipolar diagnosis, she struggled to find work and eventually burned through her savings. She had no idea where to turn until she was sent to our partner clinic.

After performing a qEEG, we discovered that she didn't have patterns associated with bipolar disorder. Instead, her symptoms were more aligned with a post-concussive syndrome, presumably from a head injury she had years ago. But while the new qEEG information helped her find treatment that cleared up her brain fog, reduced her mood swings, and got her energy levels back up, the financial and emotional damage was done. She did, however, manage to find another job, but reviving her career proved impossible.

The Financial Cost of Guessing

All of these financial costs are actually the best-case scenario, when a person with a mental health condition goes to their provider, gets a diagnosis and treatment and then hopefully starts to feel better.

But, as we've seen from the previous chapters, this often isn't the case. Patients will try a treatment and find that it doesn't work. They will then either get put on a combination of medication (each of them costing them extra), and they'll often see multiple providers and receive multiple diagnostic labels. Eventually, they may be prescribed more expensive treatments, such as transcranial magnetic stimulation (TMS) or novel psychedelics that are a large up-front payment without any guarantee of success.

Patients on a cocktail of medications may also experience negative health effects. Most drug side effects are studied individually, so it's difficult to predict the health outcomes and side effects of using several drugs at once. These health effects can again rack up indirect costs, such as lost time due to missed school and work or additional trips to the doctors.

These patients also accumulate indirect costs as they struggle to perform at work, struggle to get the help they need from families and their community, and may eventually consider the unthinkable, simply because they can't afford to spend any more on mental health care.

A 28-year old man, who used to be highly motivated and driven and had a successful engineering career, started smoking cannabis and developed a possible THC-induced psychotic break. After this break, he became incredibly unmotivated and paranoid and moved back in with his parents. He has been at home for a year and while he has a part-time job at a warehouse, he is no longer the same person he was before.

It turns out that he was using cannabis to self-medicate, because he felt he couldn't afford mental health care and didn't understand his health insurance policy. He was struggling with work and anxiety and used marijuana to alleviate these feelings. Unfortunately for him, this led to a break that has now derailed his life, which could have been avoided if he had the resources to seek professional help.

The Emotional and Social Toll

Going through a mental health crisis isn't easy. Going through a crisis, thinking you might have the solution, only to be proven wrong, is even worse. But that's what happens to many patients: they will eventually get to a point where they seek out help, and they will get a diagnosis and become optimistic about their future, only to have their hopes dashed as treatment after treatment fails.

Often, patients (especially younger patients who still rely on their parents to pay their medical bills) will feel like a burden to their family. According to Amy Wong in *Stories of Survival*, that feeling there, that you're a burden to your family, is a huge risk factor for suicide.[27]

This gets even more grim when patients start feeling like a *financial* burden. Certain treatments, like TMS, can be ruinously expensive, and not all insurance providers offer coverage. So these families are taking a large gamble for something that they're not sure will be effective. Imagine what it must feel like to know that you cost your family thousands of dollars for a treatment that didn't stick.

A 6-year-old boy displayed symptoms consistent with autism spectrum disorder, including poor eye contact, sensory processing issues, and behavioral outbursts. He was placed in special education, which limited his academic opportunities, while his parents had to deal with the stress of a lifelong condition that they thought would cripple their son.

After spending thousands of dollars on autism-related therapies that didn't help their son cope at school or home, they reached out to a partner clinic for a qEEG. The test revealed brainwave activity more aligned with auditory processing disorder and anxiety—not autism.

Armed with this knowledge, the boy underwent interventions for his condition and was later found not to meet the DSM criteria for autism. But the emotional, academic, and financial toll his inaccurate diagnosis took will always remain.

---

27 Wong, Amy, (2023) Stories of survival: the paradox of suicide vulnerability and resiliency among Asian American college students. https://doi.org/10.1093/oso/9780197662397.003.0002

The guessing game can even have an impact on society. People who can't work due to untreated or misdiagnosed mental health conditions affect their communities and larger societies too. A stark example is homeless shelters. Many people in these shelters have untreated mental conditions that prevent them from living normal lives. Moreover, people with undertreated mental health conditions are also more likely to end up in the criminal justice system, costing the taxpayer a significant amount of money.[28]

A 27-year-old man started experiencing low motivation, severe fatigue, and brain fog. He was diagnosed with depression and started a course of SSRIs that did little to help his condition. He cycled through numerous providers and was eventually diagnosed with treatment-resistant depression (TRD) and treated with electroconvulsive therapy (ECT), which also wasn't effective.

His mood continued to decline, as he started to contemplate if he was just simply broken. He started shutting down with his health care provider while thoughts of suicide crept in; he just couldn't handle the constant fatigue and fight to survive.

A qEEG revealed that he didn't have a typical depression profile and instead had a brain pattern consistent with sleep disorder-related dysfunction, potentially due to sleep apnea. After a few weeks of continuous positive airway pressure (CPAP) therapy, his mood improved, his brain fog lifted, and his suicidal ideation subsided.

---

28 Taylor, H. L., Menachemi, N., Gilbert, A., Chaudhary, J., & Blackburn, J. (2023). Economic burden associated with untreated mental illness in Indiana. *JAMA Health Forum*, *4*(10), 233535.

How much pain would he have been spared if he had obtained a qEEG at the start of his mental health journey?

The Impact on Families

Patients aren't the only ones that suffer from the guessing game. Studies show that family members who have relatives with long-term mental health conditions often also suffer from anxiety, depression, and feelings of grief.[29]

Much of this burden comes from having to provide caregiving services to the affected person, and the burden is worse for those caring for people with more severe mental health disorders. But even having to support a loved one with depression or anxiety can take a toll, particularly when the financial burden becomes a concern.

Unsurprisingly, the rate of marital conflict and chance of divorcing is higher in families that have children with ADHD or other mental health concerns compared to their peers.[30] What makes this situation worse is that children of divorced or separated parents have a higher chance of developing adjustment difficulties (such as oppositional defiant disorder or depression).[31]

---

29 Avison, W. R., & Comeau, J. (2013). The impact of mental illness on the family. In: Aneshensel, C. S., Phelan, J. C., Bierman, A. (eds) *Handbook of the sociology of mental health*. Handbooks of Sociology and Social Research. Springer, Dordrecht. https://doi.org/10.1007/978-94-007-4276-5_26 (This chapter is behind a paywall)

30 Wymbs B.T., Pelham, W.E., Jr, Molina, B.S., Gnagy, E.M., Wilson, T.K., & Greenhouse, J.B. (2008). Rate and predictors of divorce among parents of youths with ADHD. *Journal of Consulting and Clinical Psychology*, 76(5), 735–44.

31 Vousoura, E., Verdeli, H., Warner, V., Wickramaratne, P., & Baily, C.D.R. (2012). Parental divorce, familial risk for depression, and psychopathology in offspring: a three-generation study. *Journal of Child and Family Studies*, 21(5), 718–725.

This knock-on effect can be devastating, potentially resulting in a cycle of generational trauma. What's even worse is that, if the young child had been identified and treated correctly (either with medication or through environmental adjustments), their condition wouldn't have had this negative impact on their parents and the cycle may not have started at all.

A combat veteran was diagnosed with severe PTSD after presenting with anxiety, mood instability, and brain fog. His provider prescribed a range of medications including antidepressants, antipsychotics, and anti-anxiety medications, but none worked sufficiently. Not only did the veteran feel like a failure because his treatments didn't work, but he also started developing additional symptoms and felt more and more depressed.

His condition also took a heavy toll on his family life. His marriage suffered, and he felt alienated from his children. He was concerned that his mood swings would cause him to take actions he would later regret, and so he spent more and more time alone.

A qEEG showed that his brain patterns were more consistent with head trauma rather than PTSD. Once his treatment shifted away from medication and towards neurological rehabilitation, he started responding significantly better and was able to reconnect with his family.

The Cost for Providers

While patients and their families and friends bear the brunt of the toll associated with subjective psychiatry, it also affects providers.

Arguably, every provider gets into psychiatry because they truly want to help people. Often, they know people who have suffered from mental health conditions and have seen the consequences of what happens if these conditions are left untreated. But, unwittingly, providers also fall victim to the guessing game.

Providers believe that they do their best for their patients by giving them an accurate diagnosis and a treatment they expect will work based on that diagnosis. But, all too often, providers then have to watch as their patients struggle to get better, and in a further effort to help, the provider will add more medications, more treatments, and maybe modify the diagnosis. And in too many cases, these efforts don't yield any results either.

The result? Provider burnout in psychiatry is extremely high.[32] There are plenty of additional factors that contribute to burnout, including a lack of licensed mental health therapists, lack of support, and a growing disillusionment with the current state of psychiatry. More and more providers are recognizing that the DSM doesn't work and that a DSM diagnosis doesn't correlate to treatment outcome.

That's why so many providers are turning to other tools, which they hope will provide them with more objective and accurate answers. It's why, in part, so many providers are turning to psychedelics to help seemingly treatment-resistant patients.

32 Morse, G., et al. (2012) Burnout in mental health services: a review of the problem and its remediation. *Administration and Policy in Mental Health, 39*, 5, 341–352. doi:10.1007/s10488-011-0352-1

But as we've shown in the previous chapter, building these solutions on the shaky foundation of the DSM won't fix its fundamental problem of being subjective and unrooted in biological function. And so, providers, putting their hopes in these new technologies, are likely to get burned.

Summary

- An undiagnosed or misdiagnosed mental health condition can have devastating consequences for everyone involved.
- Currently, everyone in psychiatry is playing a guessing game.
- This guessing game makes all the problems of misdiagnosis and lack of treatment worse.
- The solution? Moving away from the DSM towards a more objective, biologically rooted diagnostic method.

Chapter 4

Reading the Brain

Sophie's Story

Sophie and her family had been experiencing the devastating consequences of her elusive diagnosis and failed treatment for 18 months. Mark had been suffering from burnout as he kept thinking of the number of patients he'd failed to help in his practice and struggled to cover the costs of his own daughter's treatments. The specialist bills were racking up, and Mark felt like he was drowning. And worst of all, his daughter wasn't getting better. And he couldn't think of any ways to help her using his established knowledge and experience.

Linda's questions became a constant refrain in the household, "Surely there are some more tests we can run? These checklists aren't telling us anything we don't know, and Sophie's getting worse with every new round of medication. Would an MRI help? Maybe we should get some blood work done. Just do something different, because it's obvious that the established methods aren't working."

Mark's routine cemented itself; he spent the day helping his patients while secretly wondering if he was doing any good. Then at night, he'd research alternatives to the current approach that Sophie's providers were using. Some were absolutely out there, but he discovered one that appeared promising and grounded in solid science— a brain scan method, qEEG.

His initial response was slight skepticism. There were a lot of people online saying what people wanted to hear, many miracle cures that seemed too good to be true. Was qEEG just another one of those? The last thing he wanted to do was give his wife and daughter false hope.

But as he looked deeper, he gradually became more convinced as qEEG measured brain function, identifying patterns that could be observed, recorded, and analyzed. The early literature was promising; researchers had identified multiple patterns associated with common mental health concerns such as depression, ADHD, and even treatment resistance.

As he considered the viability of qEEG, Linda's comments about testing in other fields of medicine came back to him. *We could actually see what's going on with her brain activity, rather than trying to guess based on the symptoms*, he thought. He also told himself that they had nothing to lose; traditional practices had clearly failed, and he was sick of people (himself included) trying to cure his daughter through a harrowing version of trial and error.

With trepidation and a faint glimmer of hope, Mark booked Sophie's session. The test itself was surprisingly simple and relaxed, just a few gel sensors placed on Sophie's head, a quiet room and 20 minutes of recording. Sophie almost fell asleep at one point during the closed-eyes portion. And when Mark received the results a few weeks later, he realized that the biggest mistake he'd made was waiting so long to request the qEEG.

Sophie's scan didn't clearly align with any of the diagnostic categories she'd been assigned. It didn't match what the DSM would call anxiety or depression, or ADHD. But it did match something else that we call Demand Task Cognitive Slowing (DTCS), which has recently become the focus of studies by other groups, though under a different name.[33] Instead of speeding up under pressure like most anxiety or ADHD patterns show, Sophie's brain did the opposite; it slowed down when faced with cognitive demands and created a sense of overwhelm.

The qEEG revealed frontal and central slow activity patterns that became pronounced during cognitive challenge tasks, a paradoxical response where Sophie's brain decelerated precisely when it needed to accelerate. This pattern explained why she often appeared confused or spacey during stressful situations, leading providers to assume attention deficits or dissociative symptoms.

The scan showed that it wasn't anxiety that was preventing Sophie from focusing—it was her brain's protective response to cognitive overload. When demands exceeded her processing

33 Mohamed, N., & Saleh, S. (2025). Brainwaves and higher-order thinking: An EEG study of cognitive engagement in mathematics tasks. *International Electronic Journal of Mathematics Education*, 20(4), em0852. https://doi.org/10.29333/iejme/16889

capacity, her frontal regions essentially downshifted to prevent complete overwhelm. It's actually a sophisticated adaptation, but it gets misinterpreted as psychiatric pathology.

The qEEG patterns explained why stimulant medications had made Sophie worse rather than better. Traditional ADHD medications are designed to increase arousal and focus, but Sophie's brain was already overwhelmed. Adding stimulation to an overloaded system created paradoxical effects, which included increased agitation, mood instability, and cognitive shutdown.

The brain scan analysis revealed another crucial pattern that had been completely missed by traditional assessment methods. Sophie showed the presence of mu rhythm activity, which are brain wave phenomena that typically suppress when observing others' actions, in her sensorimotor regions. In Sophie's case, the brain waves remained elevated.

When we watch someone else perform an action or express an emotion, our mu rhythm, when present, typically suppresses as our mirror neurons activate. Sophie's mu rhythm wasn't suppressing normally, which affected her ability to easily read social nuances and emotional cues.

This pattern illuminated years of social struggles that had been misattributed to various causes. Sophie's flat affect during emotional conversations hadn't been depression or dissociation, but rather it was a difficulty mirroring others' emotional states. Her difficulty understanding social subtleties hadn't been autism spectrum disorder but was a result of mirror neuron function that affected social intuition without impacting cognitive empathy.

"I always felt like I was missing something in conversations," Sophie reflected when she heard the news. "Like everyone else was getting jokes or understanding things that went completely over my head. I thought I was just socially awkward."

The findings brought a moment of profound clarity, not only for Mark, but for Sophie and Linda too. "It wasn't trauma. It wasn't bipolar. It was the patterns," he realized aloud. For the first time in 18 months, Sophie's struggles made complete neurological sense without requiring complex psychological explanations or multiple psychiatric diagnoses.

The brain scan had liberated the family from the diagnostic trap that had ensnared every previous provider. The overwhelm pattern explained her cognitive difficulties and treatment resistance. The mu rhythm findings explained her social challenges and emotional flatness. Together, these patterns painted a coherent picture of a brain working *differently* rather than a mind suffering from multiple mental illnesses. Sophie wasn't broken—she just had an unfortunate confluence of mental characteristics that were unsuited to her environment.

Mark reflected on the system that had cost Sophie some of the best years of her life. *Would we have ever found the answer? How many years of trial and error would it have taken to figure out what was going on with Sophie? Would we have ever figured out what was going on with her*?

The qEEG results also guided Sophie's treatment. While she still received some medication, the primary focus was on changing Sophie's environment, giving her plenty of space and plenty of quiet time for her brain to decompress and recharge. Some things would never change—Sophie may always struggle with social cues, and she would need more time to absorb information than her classmates—but now she understood why she was the way she was and was given individualized tools to support her.

Within a few months, Sophie's mental state improved. She became willing to socialize, had fewer mood swings, and was even starting to show interest in the hobbies she'd abandoned years before. For the first time in what felt like forever, Sophie experienced a glimmer of hope. And so did her parents. While it would take some time, their vivacious, loving daughter was coming back to them.

Mark was astonished by these developments. He'd never expected the solution to be so simple, just a short test that was noninvasive and easy to perform.

He felt revitalized and ready to practice psychotherapy again. He had a new tool in his arsenal, and while he'd always start his intakes with a few checklists to build a rapport with his patients, he understood the enormous potential of qEEG. *Now we don't have to guess; we don't have to rely on symptoms. We can look directly at the brain's activity and that can tell us so much more than our traditional methods*, he thought. Not only was he excited to start applying qEEG in his practice, but he also started thinking about ways to spread the word, starting with all the specialists that had not gotten to the root of Sophie's concerns.

What is qEEG?

An electroencephalogram (EEG) is a measurement of the brain's electrical activity that is usually obtained through attaching electrodes to the patient's scalp. These electrodes can measure electrical activity generated by surface neurons and structures deeper in the brain, like the hippocampus.

For clinical practice, EEG measures electrical frequencies, generally between 1–30 hertz (Hz), the standard unit of frequency (although the measuring tool can measure much higher and lower frequencies, these aren't used as much in practice). These frequencies are divided into four groups that tend to correspond with how awake and alert a person is. These groups are:

- **Delta waves** (0.5–4 Hz), which are pronounced while in a state of deep sleep.
- **Theta waves** (4–8 Hz), which correspond to the underlying aspects of cognition, such as learning, memory formation, and spatial navigation. These waves are abundant when a person is drowsy, lost in thought, or daydreaming.
- **Alpha waves** (8–13 Hz), which correspond to a state of relaxed wakefulness. The brain produces more of these waves when it is in a restful, calm, yet alert state.
- **Beta waves** (13–30 Hz), which correspond to a state of mental activity. They are produced when a person is thinking hard, performing challenging activities, or is deeply focused on something. They can also be associated with anxiety or excitedness.

- **Gamma brain waves** (30–80Hz), which correspond to high levels of thought and focus, such as performing difficult or challenging tasks or acquiring new and complex information.

The EEG is typically used in neurology as it can detect abnormal electrical discharges that accompany neurological dysfunction. It remains the gold standard for diagnosing epilepsy (seizures) and is frequently used to diagnose brain tumors, brain damage, encephalitis, stroke, and sleep disorders. While today's clinicians may prefer to use MRI or computed tomography (CT) scans for strokes and tumors due to the high-resolution imaging potential of these tools (which is important for discovering the location of the tumor or stroke), EEG remains a staple in the neurologist's arsenal due to its affordability, versatility, and flexibility in diagnosing neurological conditions.

A qEEG takes the analog signal (the waveforms) produced by an EEG and transforms it into digital data. This allows a qEEG to provide *a lot* more information than a traditional EEG, particularly when signals from multiple electrodes are gathered at once.

Quantitative refers to measuring or describing an object or concept in terms of numbers and generating numerical data and statistics. Quantitative research tends to be more objective than qualitative research.

> **Qualitative** refers to measuring or describing an object or concept in terms of its characteristics that may not be reduced down to numbers.

A qEEG produces a variety of metrics that are extremely useful in helping practitioners diagnose mental conditions and identify treatment options. These include the absolute power of the patient's EEG and where it is distributed in the brain, the ratio of different brain waves, the interaction and connectivity between various electrode sites, and the relative power of any of the frequency bands.

What's important to note is that certain types of deviances from these patterns are associated with potential mental health concerns. For instance, high theta activity and low beta activity correlate strongly with mind wandering, and subsequently, an elevated theta/beta ratio can be an indicator of ADHD.

The qEEG Test

The qEEG test itself is surprisingly simple considering how sophisticated the results are. The process begins with standard EEG electrode placement in 19 channels positioned according to the international 10-20 system. During the recording session, brain activity can even be observed under several different conditions:

- **Eyes-closed resting**: Baseline brain activity without external stimulation
- **Eyes-open resting**: How brain patterns change with visual input

- **Cognitive challenge tasks**: Response to attention and working memory demands
- **Recovery periods**: How quickly brain patterns return to baseline after stress

The raw EEG data undergoes artifact removal to eliminate interference from muscle tension, eye movements, and external electrical sources. Then is processed through Fast Fourier Transform (FFT) analysis to convert the analog waves to a digital signal.

qEEG as a Tool in Psychiatry

While the qEEG is routinely used in neurology and is the gold standard for epilepsy diagnosis, its value in psychiatry is currently still mostly overlooked.

Although qEEG has enormous potential, I believe one reason it remains overlooked is because it has been historically tied to the field of neurofeedback. While neurofeedback is a valuable modality, the field has long been plagued by inconsistent delivery, conflicting opinions, and the influence of self-styled gurus who don't all agree on standards. Compounding this problem, neurofeedback has not had the backing of big pharma—indeed, it often runs counter to it—so large-scale, rigorous studies have lacked funding. Because qEEG has traditionally been positioned as the gold standard entry point into neurofeedback training, its broader psychiatric value has remained limited and stuck within that narrow frame. My mission is to relieve qEEG of this burden and elevate it as an independent, evidence-driven tool for advancing psychiatric practice.

The basic idea underlying qEEG as a psychiatric tool is that varying symptom presentations are associated with distribution of brain waves that are measured in certain areas. People without symptoms typically have a standardized profile while people with symptoms will have deviations.

Most research has so far focused on individual pattern types: there is a group that looks at front alpha asymmetry, one that looks at theta/beta ratio, and several looking at various other biomarkers of potential interest. These groups have laid the foundation of associating brain patterns with symptoms that we can utilize in our own work, helping correlate certain patterns to certain trends in behavior and treatment.

Alpha asymmetry refers to the difference in alpha wave power in the left and right frontal lobes, and, while it is not typically used as a standalone marker, it is correlated with suicidality and certain types of major depressive disorder. In addition, an increase in alpha wave power in the right hemisphere is correlated with ADHD in adults and children.[34,35]

> **Suicidality** is defined as the risk of suicide indicated by suicidal intent, including attempts, and suicidal ideation, including having established suicide plans.

34 Luo, Y., Tang, M. & Fan, X. 2025. Meta analysis of resting frontal alpha asymmetry as a biomarker of depression.*npj Mental Health Research*. 4, 2.

35 Sigi Hale T, Smalley SL, Hanada G, Macion,J et al. 2009. Atypical alpha asymmetry in adults with ADHD. *Neuropsychologia*. 47 (10).

The **theta/beta ratio** is derived by dividing the theta power by beta power and has been proposed as a marker of cognitive processing capacity. An elevated theta/beta ratio is a strong biomarker for ADHD.[36] Even in people without ADHD, increased theta power and decreased beta power are observed in mind wandering episodes, further highlighting how the marker relates to attentional control.

A common way to use qEEG as an objective measurement tool is to compare a patient's qEEG values to a reference database that represents the patterns found in the population. The thinking is that the values in this database offer a baseline, and comparing the patient's readings to this baseline can help identify deviations that may be indicative of certain conditions.

We don't use this approach, largely due to the concerns about how these normative databases are constructed.[37] Also, there currently isn't an established best practice for selecting a database in our industry, and transparency surrounding database data must be improved before we are satisfied with their reliability.[38] Instead, we focus on an individual's patterns and metrics and the symptoms associated with these patterns in published literature on potential biomarkers, along with our own growing database of brain patterns.

---

36 Picken C, Clarke AR, Barry RJ, McCarthy R, Selikowitz M. 2020, The Theta/Beta Ratio as an Index of Cognitive Processing in Adults With the Combined Type of Attention Deficit Hyperactivity Disorder. *Clinical EEG Neuroscience.* 51(3), 167-173.

37 Wood, G., Willmes, K., Koten, J. W., & Kober, S.E. (2024). Fat tails and the need to disclose distribution parameters of qEEG databases. *PLoS One*, 5;*19*(1), e0295411.

38 Lorensen, T.D. & Dickinson, P. (2016). Quantitative EEG normative databases: a comparative investigation. *Journal of Neurotherapy*, 7 (3-4).

In addition to the reasons mentioned above, using an approach that focuses on individual patterns helps us avoid the problem of calling people normal or not normal. Instead, we correlate their patterns with traits, which identify both strengths and challenges facing people with those patterns.

> A **normative database** is a collection of data that represents a typical or normal population. To achieve this, producers of normative databases must ensure that they have a representative sample of the population that includes people from all ages and demographics. These databases also have strict inclusion and exclusion criteria that ensure that the database represents the norm. In most qEEG databases, people with known psychiatric or neurological disorders will be excluded. This allows providers to compare their patient's qEEG results with normal results and decide whether their results are typical or atypical (and potentially indicative of a mental health condition).

How we propose using qEEG as a psychiatric tool is to take the values derived from the 19 sites measured by electrodes and corresponding these metrics to what has been published in the field.[39,40,41] These metrics can then be used to identify patterns

39 Kopańska, M., Ochojska, D., Dejnowicz-Velitchkov, A., & Banaś-Ząbczyk, A. (2022). Quantitative electroencephalography (QEEG) as an innovative diagnostic tool in mental disorders. *International Journal of Environmental Research and Public Health*, *19*(4), 2465.

40 Leuchter, A.F., Cook, I.A., Hunter, A.M., Cai, C., & Horvath, S. (2012). Resting-state quantitative electroencephalography reveals increased neurophysiologic connectivity in depression. *PLoS ONE* 7(2), e32508.

41 Livint Popa, L., Dragos, H., Pantelemon, C., Verisezan Rosu, O., & Strilciuc, S. (2020). The role of quantitative EEG in the diagnosis of neuropsychiatric disorders. *Journal of Medicine and Life*, 13(1), 8-15.

of thought and behavior that can be useful in determining a psychiatric diagnosis.

Our proprietary software takes the patient's results and matches it to these previously published studies, which we have integrated into our algorithm. We feel this approach is more efficient than using a normative database. This algorithm can then help us predict how people are going to respond to a particular treatment as well as identify certain traits and characteristics that are backed by observed and verified data. (We try not to link our analysis to DSM-based conditions and instead emphasize the linking of patterns to traits. This will be explained in detail in the next chapter).

As we get more information from patients, our algorithm becomes increasingly refined. So initially, we can predict how one biomarker predicts treatment outcome. But with time, this can expand to three or four biomarkers that predict one medication response. We can also add new research to our algorithm as more and more researchers start investigating the connection between qEEG patterns and treatment outcomes.

We have also compiled one of the world's largest clinical databases that correlates qEEG patterns to symptoms and treatments. We've discovered that many of these patterns are stable over time: if you are an adult, your recording will be the same no matter how many tests we perform for these markers (within a reasonable range of variance, of course).

What is interesting, though, is that people's brain patterns can change after treatment. We can take a person's baseline when they first come to us, and then monitor how treatments and interventions impact the patient's brain patterns. That's the key to this entire process: that we have a way to measure progress that doesn't rely on the patient's *subjective perception* of their well-being. By focusing on environmental changes along with traditional therapies, we can create long-lasting changes in the brain and then use the qEEG to observe and measure those changes.

One of the biggest strengths of qEEG as a psychiatric tool is that it doesn't just offer a more nuanced diagnosis than the DSM. We have found that it can also strongly predict treatment outcomes based on certain biomarkers. For instance, patients with depression and higher right frontal alpha power tend to respond favorably to SSRIs,[42] whereas patients with anxiety and lower theta/beta ratios are more likely to respond to other antidepressant treatment.[43]

Criticisms of qEEG as a Tool in Psychiatry

Psychiatrists are, understandably, cautious about linking mental conditions to biological factors. We've extensively discussed how neurotransmitter theory—a hypothesis that tries to link mental health conditions to various neurotransmitter imbalances in the brain—does not tell the whole story (at best) or is a complete falsehood (at worst).

So it's understandable that clinicians may be skeptical about the value of qEEG in mental health, despite its prevalence in

42 Arns, M., Etkin, A., Hegerl, U., et al. (2015). Frontal and rostral anterior cingulate (rACC) theta EEG in depression: Implications for treatment outcome?, *European Neuropsychopharmacology*, *25*(8), 1190–1200.

43 Byeon, J., Moon, J. Y., Je, S. R., et al. (2023). Quantitative electroencephalographic biomarker of pharmacological treatment response in patients with anxiety disorder: a retrospective study. *Scientific Reports*, 13, 3802.

neurology. In this section, we'll address the most common criticisms of qEEG testing and offer our reasoning to alleviate these concerns.

DSM Categories Do Not Map onto Brain Patterns

A common criticism we hear from skeptics is that people diagnosed with the same condition, such as depression or anxiety, do not have the same brain patterns, which would imply that qEEG analysis does not follow the typical DSM categorization of mental health conditions.

This reflects how deeply ingrained the DSM is in current psychiatry, but in my opinion, this specific argument looks at the situation backward. Instead of trying to force various brain patterns into established DSM criteria, we need to move away from the subjectivity of the DSM to the objective brain patterns, which are rooted in biology, that we can now observe.

Early research shows that qEEG has plenty of value for identifying at-risk populations; as an example, in our published paper in 2023 and others, there are several potential markers for suicidality that warrant further investigation.[44,45] The results

44 Amico, F., Frye, R. E., Shannon, S., & Rondeau, S.. (2023). Resting state EEG correlates of suicide ideation and suicide attempt. *Journal of Personalized Medicine*, 13(6), 884.

45 Shamsi, F., Azadinia, F. & Vafaee, F. (2025). Association of resting-state EEG with suicidality in depressed patients: a systematic review. *BMC Psychiatry*, 25, 24.

of qEEG can also be used to predict treatment responses in anxiety,[46] depression,[47] and other psychiatric conditions.[48]

The fact that qEEG does not correlate to traditional DSM categories does not impact its ability to predict treatment outcomes. In fact, I'd argue that its ability to predict treatment outcomes is a *far more important* criterion for usefulness and practical application than mapping onto DSM categories and emphasizes the need for objective testing.

Data Gathering and Interpretation

As with all tests, the information you put in has a strong impact on your results: if you put garbage in, you will get garbage out. This is why, as we primarily focus on qEEG analysis, we need to rely on clinics around the country to send us data, and we need to be able to trust that this data is sound.

To be transparent, due to clinical limitations, some clinics send us less-than-pristine data. I believe, though, that education and standardization can help alleviate this issue.

The next thing is interpretation: Who is interpreting the data and through what lens? For instance, if you want to interpret EEGs for seizures, you must be a board-certified neurologist. At the moment, there isn't a similar qualification for qEEG and mental health. So even people with the best intentions, but

46 Byeon, J., Moon, J. Y., Je, S. R., et al.(2023). Quantitative electroencephalographic biomarker of pharmacological treatment response in patients with anxiety disorder: a retrospective study. *Scientific Reports*, 13, 3802.

47 Ip,C.T., Olbrich, S., Ganz, M., et al. (2021). Pretreatment qEEG biomarkers for predicting pharmacological treatment outcome in major depressive disorder: Independent validation from the NeuroPharm study, *European Neuropsychopharmacology*, 49,101–112.

48 Iznak, A. F., & Iznak, E. V. (2022). EEG predictors of therapeutic responses in psychiatry. *Neuroscience and Behavioural Psychology*, 52, 207–212.

who lack formal training or understanding of the underlying physiology related to this specific test, can offer qEEG testing. And that is currently a huge problem in our field.

This challenge is compounded by a well-known phenomenon: people often don't know what they don't know. Without recognizing the limits of their own expertise, they can become overly confident in their interpretations. In qEEG, that misplaced confidence can result in patients receiving misleading explanations or being directed toward treatments that don't actually fit their physiology.

To help guard against that, I've pursued the highest level of qEEG analysis certification currently available. I don't mention this to elevate myself, but to underline how critical formal training and standards are. Expertise in this area is not about claiming authority; it's about cultivating the humility to know where the boundaries are and the discipline to keep learning. My goal is to model that approach and to continue advocating for clearer guidelines and stronger oversight across the field.

We recently created a structured flow chart for interpreting qEEG data in our partner clinics. Walking a clinician through it, I asked her to identify abnormal patterns, describe the patient's symptoms from their file, and connect the two. She did very well with those tasks, demonstrating how accessible qEEG can be as a clinical tool when you have the right framework.

Prioritization is more challenging. When I asked which pattern should be addressed first, she identified two possibilities that made sense clinically, but I had already identified a different pattern as the most urgent driver. This is where advanced training and certification matter: interpreting qEEG isn't just about spotting what's abnormal or even replacing the clinician; it's about understanding what's primary and what's secondary.

The good news is that clinicians don't need to master this entire hierarchy themselves in order to use qEEG effectively. That's where our company comes in, which consists of a number of scientists, clinicians, neurologists, psychiatrists, and researchers. We've pursued the highest level of qEEG analysis certification currently available, and our role is to serve as the interpretive partner, helping clinicians make sense of the data, prioritize interventions, and avoid common pitfalls. This way, they can start using qEEG right now, with confidence, without having to become experts themselves.

Certification and minimum competency should form the bedrock of any clinical qEEG practice to avoid problems with interpretation. I think that combining human competency with computer learning is the next step in creating stronger interpretations and more useful treatment options for patients, while helping practitioners find their feet and thrive in this new landscape.

Computer analysis, like an independent component analysis (ICA) or a de-artifacting filter, will give practitioners consistent results and remove potentially irrelevant artifacts. But these filters can also go too far and cut out important data, whereas a person will keep the good information, but may be more inconsistent about removing artifacts than a digital filter.

Independent component analysis (ICA) is a computational technique in data analysis that separates and identifies independent sources of data in a mixed dataset. It can help clarify the underlying structure of a dataset by removing correlations that may otherwise hide the most relevant information.

It's important to note that while the qEEG is an objective test, it is still susceptible to some subjective interpretation. This is true of any biological test. Radiologists require years of formal training and experience before they can determine whether an image shows signs of concern that require follow-up tests or that what they're seeing is actually normal tissue.

But, what the qEEG offers psychiatrists is an objective *foundation* to build their diagnosis and treatment on, unlike the current situation where diagnosis and treatment plans are built upon a subjective interpretation of subjective "data."

Other Objective Biology-Based Tests

What makes qEEG so important is its biological basis, which can provide psychiatrists and clinicians with information about the patient's brain activity. For reference, psychiatrists and clinicians can consider other available biologically based tests in addition to the qEEG and patient interviews.

The more tools one has in their arsenal, the better the outcomes will be for everyone involved. We will look deeper at how providers can view the body as a whole rather than focusing on the brain when considering mental health in Chapter 7.

Blood Work

I think, in psychiatry, blood work—in combination with qEEG—is paramount. So many conditions that manifest as psychiatric disorders arise from problems outside of the brain. For example, thyroid issues can manifest as depression or mania, and immune system disorders can present as schizophrenia. It's vital that we take the whole body into account when looking at mental health conditions.

In my previous clinical work, we treated a young girl who presented with psychosis, but her qEEG was relatively unremarkable. When we ran her blood work and tested her gut, we discovered she had a gut infection. When we treated her with antibiotics, the psychotic symptoms disappeared. I wouldn't believe it either if I hadn't witnessed it. But these sorts of cases are routinely presented to our centers, masquerading as mental health disorders and bad behaviors.

It is helpful to recognize even a typical or expected qEEG result would be useful at this point, as a standard brain pattern can indirectly point to dysfunction elsewhere in the body. A relatively atypical brain pattern—with some mild abnormalities that don't correspond to the severity of the patient's symptoms—can be as diagnostic as one of the brain patterns we've correlated to mental health concerns. If a person is having a full-on psychotic episode but their brain patterns are relatively normal, it's a sign that the problem doesn't lie directly within the brain. Further tests, like blood work, are warranted.

Scientists and providers are starting to take a closer look at the relationship between biomarkers and mental health conditions, however they are still largely limited to the DSM categorizations. In addition to established diagnostic tools like blood work and qEEG, neurological tests are garnering some interest due to their potential in directly examining the organ we seek to treat.

Single-Photon Emission Computer Tomography (SPECT) Scan

A SPECT scan is a neurological imaging test that measures blood flow in the brain. It's used in neurology to diagnose stroke or identify the location of blood clots, but it may have some potential as a supplementary tool for psychiatric diagnosis as well. At the moment, SPECT scans offer more value as a research tool, where they can help identify the biological and biochemical basis of various mental conditions.[49]

However, there is a danger that trying to link SPECT scans to DSM-based criteria will run into the same problem that we've encountered with qEEG: that various SPECT patterns don't neatly map onto existing criteria. As with qEEG, we need to be mindful that an objective measure of patterns, traits, and characteristics underlying mental health conditions may not always correspond to the subjective collection of symptoms that underpins the DSM.

49 Kalyoncu, A., & Gonul, A. S. (2021). The emerging role of SPECT functional neuroimaging in schizophrenia and depression. *Frontiers in Psychiatry,* 15;12, 716600.

Functional Magnetic Resonance Imaging (fMRI)

While still in the exploratory stage, fMRI offers a promising way to measure brain function.[50] Unfortunately, early results are inconsistent, and the cost of fMRI makes it currently unsuitable for clinical practice. Comparatively, qEEG is significantly more affordable and reliable.

AI/Data Analysis and qEEG

A qEEG test takes the analog signal produced by an EEG and transforms it into numbers, allowing us to then analyze the data in more detail. The amount of data our clinic generates can be overwhelming. It's impossible to identify all of the relevant connections without the use of some sophisticated computational tools.

A few years ago we commissioned a data scientist to help us crunch our numbers. In our practice, we had observed that people who didn't do well on antidepressants frequently had a specific biomarker. We wanted to confirm this link with stronger data science.

The analyst asked for cases where patients had this marker and had failed three or more medical treatments. After her analysis, she identified at least four other potential markers that could contribute to the pattern as well.

The sheer number of connections that we can make is extraordinary, but we're going to need extraordinary tools to help us make sense of it all.

50 Lucas, M., Riya, P., Pütz, B., Koutsouleris, N., Müller-Myhsok, B. 2021. Systematic review of functional MRI applications for psychiatric disease subtyping. *Frontiers in Psychiatry*, 12.

The situation becomes even more complicated when we also take environmental factions into consideration. One of the things we always discuss is that brain patterns indicate traits, and the environment can determine how these traits manifest as strengths or as pathological symptoms. So AI, or data science, will continue to help us find connections between environmental factors and brain patterns as well as show us how these patterns relate to each other.

How AI Can Support qEEG

AI is becoming increasingly useful in other biologically based tests, particularly in radiology.[51] It doesn't necessarily just help us to identify connections; it can also speed up workflows, allowing clinicians and qEEG clinics to process more patients without sacrificing accuracy.

Where I really think AI will shine is when it comes to helping us untangle the complexity around suicidality. It's one of the most complex human behaviors and goes against so many instinctual safeguards that it's impossible to believe that it's connected to just a single marker. AI and data science techniques could not only help us identify the markers associated with suicidality, but also the importance and weighting of these markers. This type of research could improve our predictive capabilities, which are especially important as few of the people who attempt suicide tell anyone about their plans to do so.

With future development of an objective testing system like qEEG, we probably wouldn't even need to know anything about

51 van Leeuwen, K. G., de Rooij, M., Schalekamp, S., et al. (2022). How does artificial intelligence in radiology improve efficiency and health outcomes? *Pediatric Radiology*, 52, 2087–2093.

a person's history to predict if someone has suicidal ideation. This could be particularly useful in high-risk populations where early interventions could save lives.

At the moment, this work around suicidality is in the conceptual phase. We'd need more funding and time to perform the necessary studies to cement the work and its usefulness. But right now, we can still use qEEG and AI as ways to gather more information about suicidality and brain patterns, though not as a definitive diagnostic tool. Yet.

How AI Can Exacerbate Potential qEEG Flaws

As discussed in Chapter 2, AI can highlight and exacerbate flaws in methodology, assumptions around data gathering and analysis, and even interpretation. We also need to be extremely careful about problems like AI hallucinations and other issues that are popping up in AI at the moment, especially as we're dealing with patients and their health.

In my opinion, humans should always form a part of the qEEG testing loop, whether that is in the data collection and validation side or on the interpretation side. AI, as all other tools, needs to be used in a responsible, informed manner, making sure that we understand both its benefits *and* limitations.

Summary

- EEG is a test that measures the brain's electrical activity.
- This activity correlates to several frequencies of electrical waves that can vary across different brain regions.
- Each sensor placed on the patient's head will correspond to a particular brain location (frontal, parietal, and

temporal lobes, etc.), which in turn correspond to a particular brain function.

- The qEEG test transforms these analog waves into digital signals, which can then be analyzed.
- The brain patterns found in a qEEG strongly correlate to certain mental traits and characteristics and mental health treatment outcomes.
- By directly measuring the biological basis of mental health conditions, we can objectively test the brain.
- Removing subjectivity helps both providers and patients by reducing the need for guesswork and trial and error treatments.

Chapter 5

The Husky Phenomenon

Sophie's Story

During her experiences with traditional psychiatry, Sophie had received multiple diagnoses from depression to anxiety to ADHD. There was even one psychiatrist who suspected bipolar disorder. All of these labels had one thing in common: They focused on negative symptoms that affected Sophie's ability to function in her environment and tried to find ways to reduce the incidences of those multiple symptoms.

What Mark found most interesting about Sophie's brain scan results is that they didn't mention any DSM-based diagnosis. Sophie didn't have depression or ADHD or oppositional defiant disorder (which was yet another guess on her list of potential disorders). Instead, the analysis described Sophie's condition in terms of traits and characteristics.

The qEEG revealed that Sophie's brain was unusual. Typically, brain activity increases in response to cognitive demand. Sophie's, however, slowed down. This phenomenon, which we have coined Demand Task Cognitive Slowing (DTCS) was the reason why Sophie felt like she couldn't concentrate and would disengage and avoid doing anything that would stimulate her more.

Sophie's qEEG revealed another crucial pattern that had been completely missed by traditional assessment methods. Her mu rhythm activity showed a distinct pattern that explained years of social misunderstandings. The brain has a set of rhythms that process social information as part of the mirror neuron system, allowing people to pick up on social cues, emotional nuance, and navigate interpersonal dynamics. In Sophie's case, her brain approached social situations like an engineer trying to analyze a technical problem instead of providing intuitive social understanding.

All of these findings showed that Sophie didn't have a psychiatric disorder, as it is typically understood. She didn't have depression, ADHD, or something that could be medicated away. Instead, she had a collection of brain patterns that made life in a *traditional* school setting almost impossible. And the focus on her symptoms meant that Sophie wasn't getting the environmental support she needed; instead, her providers relied on medication to address her symptoms, in some cases exacerbating the problem due to the lack of understanding of the underlying cause.

As Mark and Linda sat Sophie down and started explaining her brain patterns and what they meant, the teenager who had been silent began to speak up for the first time in months.

"So I'm not broken?" Sophie asked quietly.

"You're not broken at all," Mark responded firmly. "You're beautifully, powerfully different. Your brain is designed for environments where deep thinking is valued, where you have time to process complex information, where your analytical abilities are assets rather than obstacles."

Sophie's eyes brightened for the first time that Mark could remember in over a year. "In the wrong environment, I short-circuited," she said slowly, testing the words. "But in the right one, I could thrive."

"Exactly," Linda confirmed. "And we're going to help you do just that."

Sophie's transformation had implications beyond her individual recovery. Her younger brother showed similar though less pronounced neurological patterns on his proactive qEEG assessment. Armed with understanding from Sophie's experience, Mark and Linda implemented environmental modifications and support strategies from the beginning rather than waiting for a crisis to develop.

The results were striking. Sophie's brother demonstrated many of the same neurological traits but never developed the academic struggles, social difficulties, or emotional challenges that had characterized Sophie's experience. His analytical nature and careful processing style were supported and channeled as a young boy, allowing them to emerge as natural strengths rather than problematic differences.

Sophie's qEEG test changed the way Mark saw psychiatric diagnosis and treatment, but it also completely changed how he viewed mental health conditions in the first place. Instead of seeing them as a collection of symptoms to be treated, he now viewed them as a reaction of certain traits to a particular environment. And in many cases, it's much easier to fix the environment than to force brain patterns into a box they aren't designed to fit.

Introducing the Husky Phenomenon

Just like Mark, qEEG changed the way I approach mental health. Instead of a set of problems to be fixed, brain patterns are biological traits that can sometimes manifest in negative ways. The way I like to talk about this is through an analogy I call the husky phenomenon.

A husky is a dog that has certain characteristics that help it thrive in its environment. It has a double coat, has loads of energy, doesn't need a lot of interaction with humans, and loves to be part of a pack.

In an Alaskan sled environment, this dog does amazingly well. It will pull the sled along with the pack, its double coat will keep it warm, and it has the drive to work all day without getting tired. It will love its life. Yes, the environment is harsh and its job demanding, but that's what the husky is best suited to do.

What do you think happens if you put that same dog in a small Arizona household as a pet? Disaster. Not only will the husky be hot and uncomfortable, it will be bored and its high energy will turn that boredom into destruction and chaos. At best, the husky will spend the whole day howling to keep itself entertained; at worst it will destroy the furniture, snap at the children, and probably get sent to a shelter.

Did the husky change? No, but its environment did.

An adolescent who had been diagnosed with depression came to one of our clinics. After a qEEG analysis, we saw that he had creative and perfectionism patterns, which are common in individuals with depression. I asked him how these patterns manifested in his day-to-day life.

He said that he used to be into running and working out, but at his new job and at school, he couldn't dedicate as much time to his workout routine as he used to. Instead, he started spending more time beating himself up about how he didn't want to exercise. He felt upset that things he used to value now felt like chores, and he was concerned that he was losing himself to his work.

What changed? His environment. Where he used to have the mental energy to pump himself up for his hobbies, this energy was now taken up by other things like work and studies.

The husky phenomenon doesn't just result in symptoms created directly from traits in the wrong environment. A whole host of problems also can arise due to maladaptive coping mechanisms.

> **Maladaptive coping mechanisms** refer to potentially harmful behaviors that a person develops to manage external or internal stressors. These behaviors temporarily relieve the person's stress, but can cause long-term harm to the person's well-being. Examples of maladaptive behaviors include substance abuse, escapism, or lashing out.

In the case of the husky, it may try to cope with boredom by giving itself a job, vocalizing, or chewing on the furniture and everything else within reach. Sheepdogs like border collies are notorious for trying to herd small children if they don't have livestock available.

In people, we see these behaviors manifest in a variety of ways. People who get overwhelmed easily may lash out or shut down. People who have high processing speeds need to move more and can get fidgety—they may start becoming disruptive if they are told to sit still—and that's when they can get labeled as defiant or disobedient.

History is full of people who very likely had aberrant brain patterns, but whose environment allowed them to express these brain patterns to the fullest potential.

Examples include:

- **Musicians and Artists**: Mozart, Beethoven, and Virginia Woolf all showed patterns of intense sensitivity, social difficulties, and cognitive differences that created struggles in conventional environments but became sources of extraordinary creative achievement when they found their optimal working conditions.

- **Scientists and Inventors**: Einstein's well-documented social challenges and unconventional thinking patterns, Tesla's intense focus and sensory sensitivities, and Marie Curie's methodical, thorough approach to research all suggest neurological differences that became competitive advantages in appropriate environments.
- **Social Analysts and Innovators:** Prominent business, technology, and advocacy leaders appear to have traits that are associated with persistent mu rhythm patterns, showing how these can drive extraordinary achievement and scientific insight. However, these persistent mu rhythms don't always translate to outward success for some, such as musician Kurt Cobain; the same patterns of sensitivity and social struggle may have fueled artistic brilliance but also profound personal challenges.

Of course, these associations are **presumed rather than proven**; none of these individuals were scanned or diagnosed using qEEG to my knowledge. They are offered here only as illustrative examples of how certain patterns might manifest in public figures whose traits are widely recognized. The key point is that deviant brain profiles, while often pathologized in psychiatry, can express themselves in positive ways.

What does the husky analogy mean for mental health providers?

It means that we need to switch up how we think about our patients. Instead of viewing them as a collection of symptoms to fix, we need to objectively measure their traits and identify the best way to shore up their weaknesses and highlight their strengths. Unfortunately, the DSM-based way of thinking is deeply ingrained and makes this shift significantly harder.

How the Psychiatric Diagnostic Systems Makes the Husky Phenomenon Worse

The goal of the current DSM is to help psychiatrists categorize a constellation of symptoms into a specific mental health disorder with the aim of prescribing a treatment to reduce these symptoms.

The husky phenomenon centers around the idea that people are a collection of traits and characteristics. If there's an environmental misfit, these characteristics can cause problems that may manifest as mental health concerns.

The DSM makes this problem worse in two different ways: First, it gives patients a label that might not even be correct (subjective interpretation of subjective symptoms). Second, by taking this approach, which reduces their characteristics to so-called problematic symptoms, we may also be significantly neglecting their strengths. Each brain pattern we measure accompanies both strengths and challenges. Just like being tall or short has advantages and disadvantages, neither are inherently good or bad.

We briefly touched on the danger of labels in Chapter 1. Patients who receive a diagnosis will start to see themselves through a particular lens, which is known as the *labeling effect*.

Other labels can introduce social stigmas, particularly with more severe diagnoses like bipolar disorder, narcissistic personality disorder, or schizophrenia. These labels can be life altering, influencing all sorts of important life decisions. Labels can affect a person's relationships with other people, their ability to find work, and even their capacity to seek help.

By reducing a patient to their symptoms and then seeking to fix these symptoms, we're trying to take a husky in Arizona and make it comfortable, either by shaving its coat (not advised), sending it to obedience classes, and maybe even getting a sand sled so it has something to do on the weekends. And if we do make physical changes, how permanent will those changes be, and do those changes address the dog's maladaptive behaviors?

In those approaches, we aren't addressing the root causes. The truth is, a husky in Arizona will never thrive—they will probably just survive.

We recently had a case in the clinic where two parents, both in high-earning professional careers, came in with their child, who they wanted to follow in their footsteps of academic excellence. The child was 10 years old when we first met him, and his parents were already talking about the colleges and higher degrees they wanted for him. The child had also been diagnosed with ADHD, and the parents wanted to know what they could do to fix him.

A qEEG revealed, unsurprisingly, that this boy had strong creative patterns, which meant he was completely unsuited to a formalized, traditional education system. He would have been far better suited in a creative field, like acting, music, or art or in an experiential type learning environment. But instead of embracing his natural tendencies or strengths, his parents responded to what they saw as a lack of potential by sending him to boarding school.

It's a sad story with no real happy ending. Instead of adjusting their child's environment such as enrolling him in an experiential learning school, for example, to meet his needs, his parents sent him away to boarding school for children with behavioral issues for the duration of his high school career (think obedience classes). Sure, the child performed okay due to the quality of the school, but did he ever thrive or realize his gifts? I don't think so.

How qEEG and Objective Testing Can Address the Husky Phenomenon

Objective testing, such as qEEG, can go a long way in shifting the way providers think about their patients. How can it do that? Objective testing removes both the subjectivity and potentially pathologizing. Instead of viewing patients as a constellation of symptoms that need to be fixed, providers can understand their patient in terms of traits and environment, which can guide treatment beyond just giving the patient medications.

In psychiatry, providers have to rely on the patient's experiences as a barometer of their improvement. They ask questions like, "Is the treatment working?" or "Are the symptoms getting better?" etc. The great thing is, qEEG results don't need the patient's subjective experience, and they provide a more objective viewpoint about the nature of each patient's concern.

We had someone come in who was suffering from depression. After the interview and qEEG, it was clear that she had distinct brain patterns of negative self-talk that were driving her other depressive symptoms. The depression was, essentially, a byproduct of the pressure she was putting on herself to find a husband and have children and her perfectionism. She was thinking about what the purpose of her life was and felt like she was failing in finding and sustaining a relationship, which affected her ability to create a family.

This patient was on SSRIs for her symptoms (the medication was not a good fit for her brain patterns), but in the context of her brain patterns, she would have been much better served by changing her perception of her value through mindfulness and talk therapy to help her cope with negative self-referencing and perfectionism.

Negative self-referencing refers to negative thoughts with reference to oneself, such as believing that a chance outcome is due to one's personal failings rather than external circumstances.

The beautiful thing about using qEEG results is that the test doesn't identify symptoms; it identifies traits that can become detrimental to a person's well-being if not supported. Negative self-referencing, for example, can in some cases be a positive trait that helps drive a person to excel and constantly improve (a high-performance athlete, for example), as long as it is balanced by mindfulness that allows a person to know when they're being too negative for their mental health.

We have seen that qEEG results can also have some predictive capabilities, helping people with certain patterns avoid situations where these patterns can become pathological.

> **Pathological**, in this instance, refers to a behavior that is uncontrolled and negative. It can also refer to symptoms of a disease (either physical or mental).

For instance, if we tested 100 children at random, it's likely that many of them would have high theta/beta ratios, which is a marker for ADHD. The skeptical psychiatrist might say, "Well, not all of these children have the symptoms of ADHD, so your test is flawed." But when you look at their environments, some parents have figured out the ideal surroundings their child needs to thrive, while others are trying to fit their children to conform to environments that aren't suited to their brain patterns (like a husky in the desert).

And the ones in unsupportive environments are undoubtedly those who present with an ADHD diagnosis.

This predictive capacity can be an important tool for mental health providers who deal with suicidality and people struggling with suicidal thoughts. In the previous chapter, we discussed how qEEG has correlated certain markers with suicidality[52] and how this could help providers identify suicidal ideation, even in patients who don't want to talk about it. Again, this is an example of how systems thinking, which is approaching mental health from the perspective of

52 Amico, F., Frye, R. E., Shannon, S., & Rondeau, S. (2023). Resting state EEG correlates of suicide ideation and suicide attempt. *Journal of Personalized Medicine, 13*(6), 884.

traits instead of symptoms, is essential. Patients who have suicidal patterns may not manifest these patterns *if* they are in a supportive environment. The predictive power of these markers is incredible.

The difficulty with suicidality is that we can't break it down into just one marker or one pattern, and the role the patient's environment plays can further complicate matters. We demonstrated this in our 2023 peer-reviewed paper.[50]

I once spoke with someone who we tested as part of a collaborative project with local first responders. During our conversation I mentioned our work on suicide prediction and afterward, this person asked if I noticed anything unusual about his analysis. I was reluctant to tell him that we'd spotted the exact suicide markers we had been studying, but eventually, I mentioned that he had some indicators of suicidality. He then told me that he'd attempted suicide 10 years before our conversation and had never shared that with anyone. What had prevented him from trying again was a significant change in his environment and psychotherapy. So while his traits remained the same, he had changed his environment to prevent the traits from manifesting.

How Moving Away from Labels Helps Patients

Taking the husky approach (considering a person's environment during evaluation) for patients offers numerous benefits. The biggest of these is that we stop overpathologizing them and instead focus on finding solutions that take advantage of their characteristics. Not only does this help move us away from problematic labels, but it also opens up a wider range of treatment options. These options focus on the patient's biology and environment rather than narrowing the focus onto the patient's symptoms.

Overpathologizing is the interpretation of normal behaviors, challenges, and emotions as symptoms of a mental health concern and as something to be fixed.

Not all brain patterns and biomarkers *need* medication. In fact, we've found that while many people have certain predispositions to specific traits, they don't display the symptoms of any DSM-based conditions.

By telling a patient that they have a certain trait, instead of a mental health condition, we empower them to take action. If necessary, we can still prescribe medication to help them manage, but we also open up a whole host of alternatives as well.

And best of all, these alternatives have a better chance of treating their brain patterns than the current approach of trial and error. The qEEG test has been shown to be a predictor of treatment response for anxiety[53] and depression[54] and, as we see in clinical practice, can do the same for many other mental health conditions. So the patient undertaking the treatment is more likely to get the results they expect.

53 Byeon, J., Moon, J. Y., Je, S. R., et al. (2023). Quantitative electroencephalographic biomarker of pharmacological treatment response in patients with anxiety disorder: a retrospective study. *Scientific Reports*, 13, 3802.

54 Iznak, A. F., & Iznak, E. V. (2022). EEG predictors of therapeutic responses in psychiatry. *Neuroscience and Behavioural Psychology*, 52, 207–212.

A potential risk of the husky approach is that it may promote discomfort avoidance. If we use qEEG in a predictive fashion, we can create situations where the environment is tailored so perfectly to the person that they don't develop any type of resilience to discomfort.

For instance, one of my children is allowed to listen to music in class, as long as his work gets done on time. This lets him stay stimulated enough to concentrate. But, would it really be so bad if he was bored for an hour? Nobody's life is completely stress-free or constantly stimulating, and learning how to deal with these negative circumstances is a part of life and a sign of healthy emotional growth.

Similarly, in an effort to avoid discomfort, people who are overwhelmed often start heavily curating their life. They start avoiding stressful situations, limit their movements and visits to places that they feel are safe, and stop trying challenging experiences.

A qEEG result can be an incentive to do that even more. If a patient knows they have a potential for getting overwhelmed and would benefit from a routine adherence, they may start panicking about anything that isn't within their routine or schedule, eventually shrinking their life to a series of small experiences that they can manage. In doing so, they limit their ability to grow and develop a stronger resilience to stress and uncomfortable situations.

However, if we make these predictions and curate the patient's environment, we still can draw clear lines to say things like, "You should still be able to cope with adversity, and experiencing some challenges will be beneficial to you."

In an ideal world, I'd like to see most children without overt mental health struggles get their first qEEG when they're 12 or 13 years old. This gives them time to live life, identify their own challenges, and potentially find ways of coping without having to depend on intense mental health interventions. And when they reach the point where they have a relatively developed brain, then we can identify their patterns and move them in a direction to best support those patterns. Their experiences can then also be beneficial, because they'll know what worked and what didn't, in addition to our guidance.

Of course, this approach wouldn't work for younger children who are already struggling. For those children, early intervention is vital to ensure they get the help they need. Again, a qEEG would be helpful in identifying their patterns and traits, discovering whether it's an environmental or biological issue that is causing their problems, and then taking the right steps to get them on the proper track as soon as possible.

An added benefit is that viewing people in terms of their traits removes a lot of the stigma associated with many of the DSM categories, particularly the more severe ones like bipolar disorder. Instead, we can refocus on the strengths of these traits. Rather than viewing someone as a person with ADHD, we can view them as creative, spontaneous people and take steps to validate these characteristics instead of reducing a person to a label such as *disruptive* or *inattentive*.

When people think about an artist like Kurt Cobain, they tend to focus on his creativity, his sensitivity, his aversion to the limelight, and his huge impact on music. But, if you were to look at him through a DSM, symptoms-based lens, he was likely bipolar with a substance abuse disorder. Both views tell the same story, but through completely different filters.

One thing I worry about is that people have a tendency to want to organize ideas into specific and potentially restrictive categories. So even with all the benefits that could come with the qEEG-based, traits-centered method I'm suggesting, what's stopping patients and providers from thinking about qEEG patterns as labels that have all the negative thinking that comes with what we currently see from the DSM method?

Hopefully, if we take a larger systems approach and encourage providers and patients to consider the fact that most people are an amalgam of a range of brain patterns (we currently report on about 12 individual markers), this will create that difference in approaching diagnoses that we're looking for. Plus, the qEEG method, combined with how the environment affects the expression of these patterns, should hopefully prevent labeling from happening. It is also my hope that this approach will change how providers view patients: no longer as a bunch of symptoms, but as a set of systems.

Brain-Based Learning Environments

The most powerful application of the husky phenomenon comes from realizing that children and teenagers do not learn in the same way.

Traditional education operates on a one-size-fits-all model that assumes all children learn optimally under similar conditions: rapid information delivery, immediate response expectations, competitive group dynamics, and standardized assessment methods. But emerging research in educational neuroscience suggests that different brain patterns require fundamentally different learning environments to thrive.

The following are alternatives that identify that people thrive in different environments. What works for one student may not necessarily work for another. They recognize that human neurodiversity needs diverse approaches and build an educational framework around that recognition.

Experiential Learning Schools that emphasize hands-on, project-based learning prove ideal for children with DTCS patterns. These environments allow students to work at their own pace, dive deeply into subjects that interest them, and demonstrate knowledge through creative projects rather than timed tests. These conditions are ideal for brains designed for sustained, thorough processing.

Waldorf Schools with their emphasis on artistic integration, storytelling, and multisensory learning provide rich, engaging environments that support both thorough cognitive processing and social-emotional development. The unhurried pace and respect for individual developmental timing matched perfectly with Sophie's neurological needs.

Democratic Schools where students have significant autonomy over their learning experiences offer the kind of self-directed, low-pressure environments where children with cognitive downshifting patterns can pursue their interests without constant performance demands.

For teachers working within traditional systems, understanding brain-based learning differences provides relief from the frustration of trying to reach students who don't respond to conventional methods. When educators realize that some children's apparent inattention or lack of participation actually reflect neurological processing differences, they can implement accommodations that support rather than fight against natural brain patterns. Even in traditional schools, progressive districts have started implementing brain-based classroom designs that include:

- **Quiet processing zones** for students who need reduced stimulation to prevent cognitive downshifting
- **Movement-friendly spaces** for children whose brains require physical activity for optimal function
- **Collaborative areas** designed for students who thrive on social interaction
- **Individual work stations** for those who need minimal distraction
- **Flexible timing** that allows students to work at their optimal pace rather than arbitrary schedules

Systems Thinking for Providers

Shifting away from symptoms towards emphasizing systems can also benefit providers. Many providers feel the pressure of the existing system, where no treatment approach comes with guaranteed results. By reducing trial and error and offering targeted therapies, qEEG-based approaches can ensure providers make more of a difference in less time and with lower costs.

Taking the husky approach is also likely to reduce the number of people in mental health crises. If people know what their brain patterns predispose them to and can take action before those traits become pathological (such as by avoiding substances, environments, and behaviors that aggravate their underlying patterns), the burden for mental health prescribers could decrease significantly with a shift on lifestyle and therapeutic interventions.

Another benefit of qEEG for providers is the reduction in people simply seeking drugs. Currently, providers have to rely on intuition and blind trust as to whether a person's symptoms are genuine or whether they're simply looking for a prescription for their go-to recreational drug. Testing with qEEG provides objective, biological information that can quickly and affordably screen these drug seekers out.

The challenge for most providers will be to break out of thinking in DSM criteria. What we've found is that there's a strong tendency for providers to look at brain patterns and say, "Oh, so that's an ADHD pattern," or "That's a depression pattern," despite how heterogenous these conditions are.

This just breaks qEEG back down into labels, and that's not what we want. We want brain patterns to correlate to strengths, not just potential symptoms. And that requires a big shift in thinking from providers.

Other medical professions never talk about the *benefits* of patient symptoms. No dentist has ever spoken about the benefits of having a cavity, because these benefits don't exist. So the husky approach is a completely different language than what most mental health clinicians and psychiatrists are comfortable using. It's going to take several shifts in thinking before this approach becomes commonplace. But qEEG testing and setting treatments according to brain patterns is a start.

DSM-based labels come with people's preconceived notions about those labels based on their experience of people with them. So, for example, my childhood knowledge of depression was developed by seeing a neighbor who would go months without leaving the house and then would snap out of it. Then he would go back to work and would be fine until another depressive episode meant we didn't see him again for six months. So when I hear that another person got diagnosed with depression, I immediately think about the neighbor across the street, because that's the context in which I know depression.

The consequence of that is that if someone says, "My daughter got diagnosed with ADHD," and you have a picture of ADHD being little boys running around going wild, they may be very skeptical about someone presenting differently. And not often discussed is that ADHD looks very different in little girls than it does in hyperactive boys. This is how labels can create a language that can build a strong bias inside the minds of people based on their previous experiences.

Another potential concern is that providers may balk at having to learn which brain patterns correlate to which treatments, especially as this is still an early and developing field. Psychiatrists and other mental health providers want to focus on helping their patients, not learning how to read qEEGs and having to relearn which treatments work for the corresponding patterns.

That's where companies like ours come in. We are gathering information with each qEEG we take, both in terms of what brain patterns correlate to which traits and which treatments have published evidence for those patterns. Our ultimate goal is to have the provider pick up our report and instantly know their patient without having to analyze or interpret qEEGs. We want them to avoid having to learn musical theory and rather just know how to play the song.

Summary

- The husky phenomenon states that huskies thrive in certain environments thanks to their characteristics, and if you take them out of that environment, they will suffer. The same principle applies to people.
- People are a collection of traits that predispose them to thrive in certain contexts and struggle in others, just as how the double coat of a husky allows it to thrive in cold environments.
- A qEEG test encourages looking at brain patterns as traits, not symptoms.
- Identifying a person's brain patterns can help us determine the best environment for them to excel.

- By changing the environment, we can prevent predispositions from becoming pathological, improving the lives of both patients and providers.

Chapter 6

Precision, Not Polypharmacy

Sophie's Story

Over the course of her treatments, Sophie took multiple medications—often at the same time. It always started the same way: the psychiatrist would prescribe one medication, and when that failed or caused unpleasant symptoms, they'd prescribe another medication to enhance the effect of the first one or to reduce the severity of the original drug's side effects.

Sophie's introduction to psychiatric medication followed the familiar pattern that has become standard practice in mental health care, not because providers prefer this approach, but because the diagnostic system traps them into it. Her initial presentation—persistent sadness, anxiety, and academic difficulties—led to a diagnosis of major depressive disorder (diagnosis code F32.9) and a prescription for sertraline, a commonly used SSRI antidepressant.

When sertraline provided minimal improvement after eight weeks, her psychiatrist was trapped into the next logical step within the system: adding bupropion to address what appeared to be inadequate antidepressant response. The combination initially seemed promising, but Sophie soon developed into increased anxiety and sleep disturbances—predictable effects when stimulating medications encounter an already overstimulated nervous system.

The third medication arrived when Sophie began experiencing emotional volatility that the system's diagnostic categories guided her psychiatrist to interpret as possible bipolar disorder. Lamotrigine was added as a mood stabilizer, despite the lack of clear manic episodes that would typically justify such a diagnosis. When Sophie complained of cognitive dulling and difficulty concentrating (side effects that could have resulted from any of her current medications), her provider suggested adding a low-dose stimulant to improve focus.

Mark didn't view this as very unusual. Prescribing multiple medications was common practice in psychiatry and accepted as the go-to option for when a single medication didn't work. However, he started noticing the negative consequences that using multiple medications had on Sophie. She started to display more and more severe side effects as the number of medications she was on increased. In many cases, these side effects were quite troubling; they included Sophie hearing buzzing noises, vertigo, brain fog, and even nerve pain and tremors.

Within 12 months, Sophie was taking five psychiatric medications simultaneously: sertraline and bupropion for depression, lorazepam for anxiety, trazodone for sleep, and lamotrigine for mood stabilization. The monthly prescription costs exceeded $800, most of which insurance declined to cover due to off-label prescribing and medication combinations lacking research support.

But the financial burden paled compared to what Mark recognized as the most troubling aspect of Sophie's treatment: the diagnostic trap had forced her provider into prescribing medications that worked in completely opposite directions, creating a pharmaceutical puzzle with pieces that didn't fit together.

- **Sertraline (SSRI)**: Increasing serotonin to boost energy and mood
- **Bupropion**: Stimulating dopamine and norepinephrine systems
- **Lorazepam**: Sedating Gamma-Aminobutyric Acid (GABA) systems to reduce anxiety
- **Trazodone**: Blocking serotonin receptors to induce sleep
- **Lamotrigine**: Stabilizing neural membrane excitability

The result was neurochemical chaos where Sophie's brain received contradictory signals simultaneously. Her overwhelm phenotype—already struggling with sensory regulation and arousal control—was being pushed and pulled by medications working at cross-purposes.

Following Sophie's qEEG results, she was prescribed one medication and a lifestyle treatment, which surprised Mark. No multiple drugs, no combination of therapies and treatments—

just a single drug and lifestyle modifications that were easy to administer, affordable, and readily available. And best of all, Sophie's mood started improving almost immediately, and within a few months she was well on her way to recovery.

In medicine, polypharmacy refers to the use of five or more medications to treat a single condition. In psychiatry, polypharmacy is more narrowly defined as the use of two or more psychiatric drugs to treat a mental health condition.[55,56]

Polypharmacy comes in a variety of forms including:

Same-class combinations: Using multiple medications from the same category, such as combining two different SSRI antidepressants or prescribing multiple benzodiazepines for anxiety management

Multi-class targeting: Employing medications from different categories to address the same symptoms, such as combining antidepressants with antipsychotics for depression treatment

Side-effect management: Adding medications specifically to counteract adverse effects of primary treatments, creating cascading prescription patterns that can become self-perpetuating

Symptom-specific additions: Prescribing additional drugs to address new symptoms that emerge during treatment, often without being able to determine whether these symptoms

55 Kukreja, S., Kalra, G., Shah, N., & Shrivastava, A. (2013). Polypharmacy in psychiatry: a review. *Mens Sana Monographs*, 11(1), 82–99.

56 Medical Directors Council and State Medicaid Directors. Alexandria, Virginia. (2001). National Association of State Mental Health Program Directors: Technical Report on Psychiatric Polypharmacy.

represent disease progression, medication side effects, or drug interactions

Polypharmacy is common clinical practice for many psychiatrists, and its incidence has been rising steadily. A recent study found that 68.2% of children experiencing severe mental health symptoms were on two or more medications, and typically, patients with ADHD or anxiety tended to receive more medications overall.[57]

Psychiatry's tendency towards polypharmacy is a direct result of the guessing game because DSM categories do not provide any predictions of treatment efficacy. Providers have to work out their own solutions from experience, and treatment becomes more of an art than a science. And when all options fail, the next reasonable step is to try several medications at once, either to enhance the effectiveness of the treatment or to tackle the problem from multiple angles.

The situation is made worse by the fact that it's very hard to tell, objectively, whether a certain medication is working. Providers need to rely on subjective patient reviews and base their evaluation of the treatment's effectiveness on indicators that are subjective and variable. Patients may feel better one day, but feel worse the next, and they may attribute this to their medications. This leads to providers prescribing new medications to address these seemingly worse feelings.

---

57 O'Brien, M. J., Pauls, A. M., Cates, A. M., Larson, P. D., Zorn, A. N. (2024). Psychotropic medication use and polypharmacy among children and adolescents initiating intensive behavioral therapy for severe challenging behavior. *The Journal of Pediatrics*, 271, 114056.

How Polypharmacy Affects Patients and Providers

Research on psychiatric polypharmacy can make for disturbing reading. Not only does polypharmacy increase the risk of adverse drug reactions threefold when compared to monopharmacy, but it also extends the duration of treatment and has no clear advantage over monotherapy.[58]

Monopharmacy and **monotherapy** refer to the practice of prescribing one drug or applying one therapeutic intervention, respectively.

For patients, this means worse side effects, a longer amount of time before they feel better, and uncertainty about the likelihood of getting better. It also means having to pay more each month for medication that may not work while these differing medications may contribute to permanent negative impacts on their life.

The biggest problem surrounding polypharmacy is that almost all drug safety trials are on one drug alone. So while we know the safety and efficacy of a particular drug when it is used on its own, we have no idea what's going on when we combine it with another drug. At this point, psychiatrists have to rely on clinical series and expert opinions or venture out into the wild unknown and hope for the best.

58 Stassen, H. H., Bachmann, S., Bridler, R., Cattapan, K., Herzig, D., Schneeberger, A., & Seifritz, E. (2022). Detailing the effects of polypharmacy in psychiatry: longitudinal study of 320 patients hospitalized for depression or schizophrenia. *European Archive of Psychiatry and Clinical Neuroscience, 272*(4), 603–619.

A **clinical series** is a type of observational study design that describes the experiences of a (typically) small group of people, usually during a medical intervention for a particular condition. The key feature of a clinical series is that the researchers don't control the intervention, but simply describe what happened to the patients undergoing it.

For instance, a clinical series on depression may track patients who have undergone a novel therapy and describe their results, but the study and researchers aren't the ones performing the novel intervention.

As with everything in medicine there are no absolutes, and there is at least one instance where polypharmacy has been tested extensively and shown to be more effective than monotherapy. This exception is manic episodes in bipolar disorder, where several papers show the effectiveness of prescribing lithium with second-generation antipsychotics.[59,60]

Mental health providers don't choose polypharmacy because they prefer complex treatment regimens or enjoy managing multiple medication interactions. They become corralled into this approach because the diagnostic system provides inadequate tools for precise decision-making. Given the limitations of current diagnostic frameworks, polypharmacy

59 Yatham, L. N., Paulsson, B., Mullen, J., & Vagero, A. M. (2004). Quetiapine versus placebo in combination with lithium or divalproex for the treatment of bipolar mania. *Journal of Clinical Psychopharmacology*, 24, 599–606.

60 Sachs, G., Grossman, F., Okamoto, A., et al. (2002). Risperidone plus mood stabilizer versus placebo plus mood stabilizer for acute mania of bipolar disorder: a double-blind comparison of efficacy and safety. *American Journal of Psychiatry*, 159, 1146–1154.

often represents logical clinical reasoning within a fundamentally flawed system that constrains even excellent providers into relying on incomplete information.

Polypharmacy also has significant drawbacks for providers, with the big one being, of course, liability. Combining several treatments can lead to unexpected side effects that reflect directly back to the provider's prescription. This is particularly important when providers start prescribing off-label medications (medications not intended to treat a particular condition), which makes issues of liability a lot murkier.

Another problem is that polypharmacy can muddy the waters in a way that keeps providers from knowing which drug is actually doing the heavy lifting. If a patient is on five drugs for one condition, how can their team know which one is working, which one is harming, and which one is having no effect? Patients may even experience new symptoms from drug interactions that may be misinterpreted as a worsening of their condition, leading to even more medications or treatments that are unnecessary at best or harmful at worst.

I can completely understand why mental health providers revert to polypharmacy, considering the limited tools they have at their disposal. Not only do they have to guess at potential treatment options based on a subjective diagnosis, but they also have to rely on the patient's subjective interpretation of whether the treatment is working as intended or not. And, considering how heterogenous most DSM conditions are, it's no surprise that most patients end up taking multiple drugs to address their symptoms.

qEEG Promotes Precision

A qEEG is a brain scan that provides objective information about a person's brain patterns. And these brain patterns correlate extremely well with treatment response[61]—to the point where we can say that a person with this type of pattern won't do well on SSRIs, but may do well on Drug X instead. While early research demonstrates that qEEG patterns can predict antidepressant response with a remarkable 70–80% accuracy—significantly surpassing the 30–40% success rate associated with traditional psychiatric methodologies—it stands to reason that when this objective data is combined with the nuanced insights gained from a provider's extensive clinical experience, the predictive accuracy should ascend even higher, likely exceeding 90%.[62] This integration of robust biomarker data with seasoned professional judgment offers a more precise and individualized approach, moving beyond probabilistic guesswork toward a truly targeted intervention.

What this means for patients and providers is clear: instead of guessing what medication to give, with the help of qEEG results the provider can map out and create a clear treatment plan. Better yet, qEEG analysis can then be used to measure the treatment's effectiveness without needing to rely only on the patient's subjective interpretation of their feelings.

---

61 Byeon, J., Moon, J. Y., Je, S. R., et al. (2023). Quantitative electroencephalographic biomarker of pharmacological treatment response in patients with anxiety disorder: a retrospective study. *Scientific Reports*,13, 3802.

62 Bruder, G. E., Sedoruk, J. P., Stewart, J. W., McGrath, P. J., Quitkin, F. M., & Tenke, C. E. (2008). Electroencephalographic alpha measures predict therapeutic response to a selective serotonin reuptake inhibitor antidepressant: pre- and post-treatment findings. *Biological psychiatry, 63*(12), 1171–1177.

Results from a qEEG analysis are also useful in helping patients with multiple, complex patterns to tease out which symptoms are due to brain patterns (hardware) and which are environmental (software). If you've addressed a patient's atypical patterns with the appropriate treatment and they're still showing symptoms, you'll know that the likely culprit is the environment, which eliminates the temptation to pile on more medication unnecessarily.

After undertaking the interventions recommended in his initial report, a patient came back to us saying that he still had struggles in one particular area. And what we saw is that he had gotten as far as medication and treatment could take him, as far as changing his brain could take him; the next step was to work on his relationships, his job, and his environment overall.

We now know that qEEG can be incredibly useful for separating the signal from the noise and finding the way forward for patients—who would otherwise be classed as treatment-resistant—without having to resort to polypharmacy.

A biomarker-driven approach is also likely to affect psychiatric research and medicine development, encouraging pharmaceutical companies to develop new, more targeted drugs. At the moment, pharmaceutical treatments are aligned with the DSM, which by now we've seen leads to guessing and polypharmacy. This isn't to say we need *more* drugs, instead we need a more precise, objective-data driven application of drugs that are already available.

Biomarker-driven studies offer an exciting new avenue that enables companies to develop treatments specifically tailored to a particular biomarker. So instead of a drug having a 60% efficacy for depression, the drug could be targeted with 95% efficacy to treat based on the results of a particular biomarker. And unlike previous studies that relied on checklists and subject feedback to validate the results, qEEG analysis could objectively quantify the drug's usefulness.

So ultimately, qEEG and other biomarker-based testing could drive precision through the development of new treatments made to address particular patterns. While this wouldn't eliminate polypharmacy entirely—certain people may need two drugs with synergistic effects as we saw in the example for bipolar disorder—it would dramatically reduce the amount of medicine typical psychiatric patients take. This type of change can only help the providers and patients in the psychology and psychiatry worlds.

The Benefits of Precision

The main benefit of precision for patients is that it reduces the potential for adverse side effects or negative interactions between various drugs. It also makes treatment significantly more affordable.

In addition, employing precision means that patients don't need to spend months or years trying out various treatments before finding out which one works for them. We can tailor their interventions immediately based on their brain patterns. We then carry on monitoring their brain patterns to ensure the treatments work as expected so that we can make even more precise adjustments (if needed) along the way.

For example, if you needed a suit, you could go into a store and try one off the shelf. If that one doesn't fit, you wouldn't just try to find a second one to put on top of it to see if it looks alright. And while the first suit might cover your skin, perhaps it still doesn't really fit in all the right places. The second suit fits even worse, and now you have the issue of how that suit conflicts with the first one. Polypharmacy is just throwing on suits on top of other suits, hoping that something fits and wondering why suddenly you look like a rumpled mess. Alternatively, qEEG is like visiting a tailor who will get all of your measurements and design a bespoke suit that looks great and fits you specifically.

Many psychiatric interventions take months to really have an effect. If parents don't want to medicate their anxious child, they'll first try talk therapy. But, if they spend six months in therapy without a result, that's a lot of time wasted particularly for a young child. But if we had the right, proven treatment plan from the outset, we could have directly started medications without trying therapy first, because we know what the root cause is and tailored their therapy to their individual needs.

Precision also benefits providers. Not only does it reduce the potential for liability and harm that may arise from polypharmacy, it also gives them confidence that what they're doing will work. Having a precise understanding of the patient's brain patterns can help the provider determine whether the problem is hardwired, environmental, or something completely different. I like to think about it as hardware (brain pattern) versus software (environment)—both can contribute to a problem and require different solutions, either changing the software to fit with the hardware or fixing the hardware.

Plus, qEEG doesn't always need to provide positive results to be useful. The absence of atypical brain patterns can be just as telling. If a person is showing symptoms of psychosis but their qEEG results are only mildly atypical, it can be a strong indicator that further testing, such as other lab testing or blood markers, needs to be done.

Summary

- Current psychiatric practice encourages polypharmacy: the use of multiple medications to treat a condition.
- Polypharmacy can lead to a host of problems, including an increased risk of side effects and adverse reactions.
- At the same time, polypharmacy is unlikely to offer commensurate mental health benefits. Patients do not improve faster on multiple medications.
- Mental health providers resort to polypharmacy as a consequence of having to guess at treatments due to the subjective nature of the DSM.
- Results from a qEEG promote precision by clearly linking treatments to specific patterns.
- Objective testing can also distinguish between biological and environmental causes of mental health symptoms.

- The biomarker-driven approach helps providers immediately select the best treatment for a patient without the need for guessing.
- Precision reduces the chance and severity of adverse reactions.
- Having the ability to more reliably match treatment to brain pattern also reduces the time it takes for patients to see a positive response to treatment.

Chapter 7

The Mind as Part of the Body

The Mind and the Body

Most people assume that there is a clear distinction between mental and physical illness and that mental illnesses originate in the brain or mind, while physical illnesses originate from other organs or biological processes.

But the situation is much more complex and nuanced. Certain diseases, such as epilepsy, stroke, and brain cancer, are clearly diseases of the brain, but they don't necessarily have a primary mental health component. And not all mental health illnesses are caused by brain dysfunction, they can instead stem from problems in other parts of the body.

In this chapter, we're going to take a closer look at a more full body approach to mental health from a perspective that doesn't solely look at symptoms or the brain. We'll examine how qEEG and testing the brain play a vital role in psychiatric care. We'll also highlight that it would be unwise to limit one's viewpoint to simply the brain when thinking about mental health and psychiatry.

This change in approach doesn't only affect how providers practice, but is also beneficial for patients and the parents of young patients. If patients know that not all mental health conditions aren't caused by the brain, they can ask more supportive questions that can help them and their provider work better together to identify the underlying cause of their condition sooner.

Not All Mental Health Conditions Stem from the Brain

Mental illness isn't just a symptom of a broken or dysfunctional brain. Biological factors, like a person's genetics, certain infections, or chronic health conditions, can all influence a person's mental health. Similarly, socioeconomic and environmental factors can play a huge role in how people respond to stress. It's well-known that poverty and social isolation contribute to mental illness.[63,64]

Reducing these conditions to a set of psychiatric symptoms leaves a lot of room to miss the root causes of the patient's concerns.

Before moving to qEEG analysis full time, I worked and lived in a world where most psychiatric conditions were medical and not mental, until proven otherwise. Someone would come in with ADHD, and we'd do a whole panel of tests, looking at

---

63 Knifton, L., & Inglis, G. (2020). Poverty and mental health: policy, practice and research implications. *BJPsych Bulletin, 44*(5), 193–196.

64 Saltzman, L. Y., Hansel, T. C., & Bordnick, P. S. (2020). Loneliness, isolation, and social support factors in post-COVID-19 mental health. *Psychology and Trauma,12*(S1), S55-S57.

their thyroid hormone levels, food reactions and diet, their sleep patterns, and even their gut biome. We'd look at their environment and see whether they were doing supportive things for their brain patterns or whether they were engaging in self-destructive behaviors. And the qEEG analysis would only be part of a suite of tests that looked not just at the brain, but at the whole body.

And this is where qEEG really shines: It tests the brain and its activity, and if it doesn't yield a plausible explanation for the person's mental illness, it's time to look at the rest of the body.

Common Physical Conditions with Mental Health Symptoms

Thyroid Disease

Thyroid disease is closely linked with mental symptoms as well as physical symptoms. For instance, an underactive thyroid can lead to cognitive and processing problems like brain fog, memory lapses, and lack of mental alertness. It can also cause or exacerbate mental conditions like depression.

Patients with an overactive thyroid may experience anxiety, irritability, and strong mood swings. Typically, the more severe the thyroid condition, the more severe the mental health symptoms.

Luckily for practitioners, thyroid conditions rarely manifest as just psychological symptoms and are often associated with many other physical symptoms, such as weight loss or gain, temperature sensitivity, shakiness, or fatigue. However, if a patient experiences treatment-resistant depression (TRD) or anxiety, checking their thyroid stimulating hormone levels may be something to consider.

Thyroid blood tests will often test for a panel of hormones and proteins, including thyroid stimulating hormone (TSH), thyroid hormones T3 and T4, and thyroid antibodies that can indicate an autoimmune disorder.

Allergies

There is a growing body of evidence that shows links between allergies and mental health conditions such as depression and anxiety.[65,66] The mechanisms behind these links vary depending on the allergy and mental health condition. Some researchers speculate that the inflammatory response behind an allergic reaction also affects the brain, resulting in a predisposition for conditions like depression and anxiety.

Allergic reactions are often stressful, leading to the production of the stress hormone, cortisol, which can affect mental health. Similarly, many allergic reactions cause visible marks, which can cause social isolation, another risk factor for mental health concerns.

The challenge with allergies is knowing which one comes first: Is the allergy causing the mental health problem, or is there an underlying factor that contributes to both? Studies show that reducing allergies improves mental health in most

---

65 Amritwar, A. U., Lowry, C. A., Brenner, L. A., Hoisington, A. J., Hamilton, R., Stiller, J. W., & Postolache, T. T. (2017). Mental health in allergic rhinitis: Depression and suicidal behavior. *Current Treatment Options in Allergy*, Mar; *4*(1), 71–97.

66 Conway, A. E., Verdi, M., Kartha, N., Maddukuri, C., et al. (2024) Allergic diseases and mental health. *Journal of Allergy and Clinical Immunological Practice,12*(9), 2298–2309.

patients,[67] but it's almost impossible to know whether this is due to changing their underlying physiology or simply making the environment around them more supportive.

Abnormal Lipid Utilization

Lipids, or fats, are an essential component of brain function. They form the myelin sheath around neurons, are essential in neuroplasticity, and may act as neurotransmitters.

> **Neuroplasticity** is the brain's ability to change its structure and function to adapt to experiences by forming novel connections and breaking old ones. It is the foundation of picking up knowledge and learning new skills.

There is a strong link between brain lipids and mental health conditions like schizophrenia, bipolar disorder, and depression.[68] However, there is also a growing link between lipid utilization—or how lipids are metabolized and used in the body—and depression[69] and ADHD.[70]

67 Conway, A. E., Verdi, M., Kartha, N., Maddukuri, C., et al. (2024) Allergic diseases and mental health. *Journal of Allergy and Clinical Immunological Practice,12*(9), 2298–2309.

68 Schneider M., Levant B., Reichel M., Gulbins E., Kornhuber J., Müller C.P. (2017). Lipids in psychiatric disorders and preventive medicine, *Neuroscience & Biobehavioral Reviews*, (76), 336–362.

69 Luan, X., Wang, X., Shi, Y., Zhang, X., Wang, Y., Zhou, M., Wu, Z., Liu, Z., Li, X., Zhang, L., Shao, T., Chen, R., Chu, X., & Wei, H. (2025). Abnormalities of lipid metabolism in the progression and treatment of depression. *Frontiers in Psychiatry*, 16. https://doi.org/10.3389/fpsyt.2025.1589663

70 Xu, Y., Bao, L., & Liu, C. (2021). The relationship between blood lipid and attention-deficit/hyperactivity disorder (ADHD) in an obese population of Chinese children: an obesity-stratified cross-sectional study. *International Journal of General Medicine*, 14:10503-10509.

What we also see is children with blood panels showing elevated lipids (particularly total cholesterol and low-density lipoproteins). The children themselves have low energy levels, low muscle tone, and sometimes what is referred to as chicken skin (keratosis pilaris) on the back of their arms. They will present with ADHD or have learning disorders. In reality, their real problem is that their body isn't using their lipids properly, sometimes due to a metabolic disorder and sometimes due to genetics or lifestyle factors (like being sedentary). We see this a lot with stimulant-resistant ADHD children: the stimulants don't do anything because the fundamental problem is that the brain (and body) don't have the energy to work.[71]

Infection

In the practice, I've seen a whole subgroup of people whose psychiatric symptoms are caused by initially acute, but later chronic, infection. These infections can be bacterial, viral, or even fungal in nature. It's uncertain whether the link is between the pathogen and the condition or whether it's the body's immune response that has gone haywire and started attacking the brain, causing psychological symptoms.

Pediatric autoimmune neuropsychiatric disorders associated with streptococcal infections (PANDAS) is a relatively new diagnosis that highlights the connection between the body's response to a *Streptococcus* infection and neurological and

71 Schneider M., Levant B., Reichel M., Gulbins E., Kornhuber J., Müller C.P. (2017). Lipids in psychiatric disorders and preventive medicine, *Neuroscience & Biobehavioral Reviews*, (76), 336–362.

psychological symptoms, showcasing how our nervous system is impacted by the immune system.[72]

Some children can develop obsessive-compulsive-like symptoms, tics, and ADHD-like symptoms that start and then resolve, only to restart again in a few weeks. When you ask about their recent medical history, many of them have had chronic strep throat infections or acute scarlet fever in the weeks leading up to their first episode.

We were contacted by a psychiatrist in a residential school about a child who had angry outbursts and ADHD symptoms. None of the medications they had tried had worked, and the child was struggling in the academic setting.

After a qEEG showed relatively typical brain patterns, we started running other tests. One of these was a urine test looking at his gut microbiome, and we noticed that he had an abnormal amount of yeast markers. We treated him with a common antifungal and within a few days his behavior and concentration had improved so much that we got a call from the school psychiatrist asking what we'd prescribed. They couldn't believe it when we told him that it was a simple oral antifungal as the change was so rapid and so dramatic.

When I was in clinical practice, I often saw people who had latent, untreated viral infections, like Epstein-Barr virus, that

72 Wayne, C. R., Bremner, L., Faust, T. E., Durán-Laforet, V., Ampatey, N., Ho, S. J., Feinberg, P. A., Arvanitis, P., Ciric, B., Ruan, C., Elyaman, W., Delaney, S. L., Vargas, W. S., Swedo, S., Menon, V., Schafer, D. P., Cutforth, T., & Agalliu, D. (2023). Distinct Th17 effector cytokines differentially promote microglial and blood-brain barrier inflammatory responses during post-infectious encephalitis. https://doi.org/10.1101/2023.03.10.532135

come to the clinic with psychiatric symptoms. Once we ruled out psychological and neurological conditions with the qEEG, we could look at other markers, usually through blood work or other physiological tests.

One of the earliest patients in the clinic was a 3-year-old child who had been controversially diagnosed with bipolar disorder at the local children's hospital. The child's mother came to us because she didn't want to put her child through the treatment that went along with that diagnosis. I remember him like it was yesterday: He was biting and scratching his mother, and this poor, innocent mom was at her wits' end.

If we went by symptoms, the child was absolutely matching bipolar symptoms, and his behavior warranted the treatment proposed. But, instead, we looked at other physical markers. In this instance, we didn't run a qEEG, because we didn't have enough information about 3-year-old brain patterns to get any useful data from that analysis. Instead, we looked at his blood work and gut markers and saw that he had a chronic gut infection with a common bacteria.

After a round of antibiotics and changes to his diet, which corrected his gut microbiome, the boy got significantly better. He ended up needing several treatments due to the difficulty of maintaining the nutritional recommendations needed to support his gut biome, but the link between his mental health and gut health were very clear.

Autoimmune Conditions

Research shows a significant overlap between autoimmune conditions, such as celiac disease, and psychiatric symptoms.[73] Conditions such as Grave's disease, multiple sclerosis, and lupus often present with symptoms ranging from depression and anxiety to psychosis.

Autoimmune conditions can be difficult to diagnose at the best of times; they often flare up and then fade away, resulting in a varying presentation that can confound even specialists. A recent study showed that a psychiatric misdiagnosis of an autoimmune condition can have significant and lasting impacts on patient lives, including exacerbating their symptoms and decreasing their trust in the health care system.[74]

A 32-year-old woman was referred to us by her mental health provider due to treatment-resistant anxiety. The woman had tried four medications with no results, and a qEEG test showed that she didn't have any anxiety markers. However, blood work showed positive celiac disease markers and elevated inflammation markers.

We recommended a gluten-free diet, and within three months the woman reported that her anxiety had significantly decreased. After six months of the diet, the woman's anxiety was no longer a psychiatric concern.

---

73 Alkhiari, R. (2023). Psychiatric and neurological manifestations of celiac disease in adults. *Cureus, 15*(3), e35712. doi:10.7759/cureus.35712

74 Ravan, J. R., et al. (2021). Autoimmune rheumatic diseases masquerading as psychiatric disorders: a case series. *Mediterranean Journal of Rheumatology*, 2, Convin SA, 164.

Nutrient Deficiencies

Most people tend to regard nutrient deficiencies as something that doesn't really happen in the modern world, but these deficiencies can have devastating consequences on a person's health and mental well-being.

The growing trend of high-calorie, low-nutritional foods that are affordable, tasty, and quick to prepare has led to an increase in vitamin and nutrient deficiencies in the US.[75] These deficiencies not only affect a person's physical health and well-being, but also their mental state. Studies show that deficiencies in nutrients such as proteins, magnesium, selenium, vitamins B12 and D, and zinc can affect brain and nervous system function, mimicking the symptoms of depression.[76]

For instance, vitamin B12 deficiency often comes with distressing psychiatric symptoms, including psychosis, dementia, anxiety, and depression. It can also cause brain fog, insomnia, and visual hallucinations.[77] This is particularly concerning as vitamin B12 deficiency is surprisingly common in vegans and vegetarians.[78]

---

75 Reider, C. A., et al. (2020). Inadequacy of immune health nutrients: Intakes in US adults, the 2005-2016 NHANES. *Nutrients, 12*(6), 1735. 10 Jun. 2020, doi:10.3390/nu12061735

76 Zielińska, M., et al. (2023). Dietary nutrient deficiencies and risk of depression (Review Article 2018-2023)." *Nutrients, 15*(11), 2433. 23 May. 2023, doi:10.3390/nu15112433

77 Ankar, A., & Kumar, A. (2025) Vitamin B12 deficiency. [Updated 2024 Sep 10]. In: StatPearls. Treasure Island, Florida: StatPearls Publishing; 2025 Jan-. Available from: https://www.ncbi.nlm.nih.gov/books/NBK441923/

78 Niklewicz, A., Smith, A. D., Smith, A., Holzer, A.,et al. (2023). The importance of vitamin B12 for individuals choosing plant-based diets. *European Journal of Nutrition*, 62(3), 1551–1559.

A 72-year old woman came to us complaining of depression and memory lapses that started in the past year. Her primary care provider prescribed sertraline, but the patient found the side effects to be deeply unpleasant and wanted a second opinion.

Blood work revealed that her vitamin B12 levels were well below the normal range. A simple B12 supplement was enough to alleviate her depression and improve her memory dramatically.

Similarly, a magnesium deficiency can manifest as depression. Magnesium is essential for controlling certain brain chemicals such as GABA, serotonin, and glutamate, which all affect mood and sleep regulation.[79]

Omega-3 fatty acids have received a lot of attention due to their health benefits, which include reducing triglyceride levels in the blood and lowering the risk of certain cancers and dementia. However, there are some studies that also implicate omega-3 fatty acid deficiency in depression due to a decrease in neural function.[80] Other studies show how omega-3 fatty acid supplementation can be a useful adjunctive strategy in treating depression.[81]

---

79 Eby, G. A., Eby, K. L., & Murck, H. (2011). Magnesium and major depression. *Magnesium in the Central Nervous System*, 313–332. https://doi.org/10.1017/upo9780987073051.024

80 Sinclair, A., Begg, D., Mathai, M., & Weisinger, R. (2007). Omega 3 fatty acids and the brain : Review of studies in depression. Deakin University. Journal contribution. https://hdl.handle.net/10536/DRO/DU:30007690

81 Raza, M. L., Hassan, S. T., Jamil, S., Fatima, W., & Fatima, M. (2025). Nutritional interventions in depression: the role of Vitamin D and omega-3 fatty acids in neuropsychiatric health. *Clinical Nutrition*, 45, 270–280. https://doi.org/10.1016/j.clnu.2025.01.009

The qEEG and a Whole-Body Approach to Psychiatry

The Electrical-Biochemical-Behavioral Connection

The qEEG helps us see how the brain is performing, but brain activity does not exist in a vacuum. Body chemistry—hormones, nutrients, immune system, and metabolic status—can shift neural signaling and, in turn, behavior. In other words: biochemistry influences electricity, and electricity influences behavior.

So how does this impact the provider who needs to navigate this connection? A working model may start with stabilizing the biochemical foundation through:

- Restoring key cofactors and neurosteroids through vitamin D, magnesium, and zinc supplementation, as well as addressing vitamin B12 and iron if blood work shows levels to be low.
- Reducing neuroinflammation through omega-3 fatty acid and curcumin supplementation
- Supporting the gut—brain axis and optimizing nourishment by assessing dysbiosis, emphasizing fiber- and polyphenol-rich whole foods, ensuring adequate protein, and considering targeted probiotics and digestive support when indicated.
- Supporting metabolic energy and lipid handling through adequate protein intake and addressing dyslipidemia when present.

Dyslipidemia refers to an unusually high or low amount of lipids in the blood.

The goal of this step is to stabilize the cortical rhythms by ensuring that the body's membranes, neurotransmitters, and immune system are normalized. Sometimes, if the patient suffers from a nutrient deficiency, this may be sufficient to resolve their psychiatric symptoms.

If not, the next step is to support electrical optimization through:

- qEEG-informed neurotherapies
- Autonomic nervous system training, such as breath and heart rate variability (HRV) work, to restore flexible stress responses
- Sleep consolidation, such as screening and treating sleep apnea or applying Cognitive Behavioral Therapy for Insomnia (CBT-I) principles, to allow neural recovery

The final step is to integrate behavioral interventions to ensure that the patient's cognitive and skills strategies are matched to their measured brain patterns (think, the husky in the desert). A large part of that process is to ensure that the patient's environmental modifications accommodate their neurotype.

This working model represents the future of mental health care. Instead of treating surface symptoms with psychiatric medications, we can identify and address the physiological factors that overwhelm neural networks. Instead of accepting that some people are just seen as treatment-resistant, we can investigate why their brains can't maintain optimal function.

Many people labeled with psychiatric disorders are actually experiencing normal brain responses to abnormal physiological conditions. When we optimize the biochemical foundation, the electrical patterns normalize, and the behavioral symptoms resolve naturally.

The Role of qEEG in Integrative Medicine

I firmly believe that qEEGs with objective biomarkers are the future of psychiatry. They give us insight into the physical source of mental health conditions, providing us with objective data instead of forcing us to rely on symptoms and the patient's subjective experience.

However, there are limits to what the qEEG can do, especially in the context of the whole-body approach. There are many confounding factors that can influence a person's mental health, and the qEEG can't detect them all.

You may hear some proponents of qEEG say that they can pick up so-called thyroid patterns or say that heavy metal poisoning has certain trends. I recently saw a study that suggests that a very specific pattern (beta spindling) is indicative of benzodiazepine use.[82] But the problem with these claims is that many of these markers are nonspecific. A qEEG result showing global slowing (a relatively common qEEG abnormal pattern) can indicate opiate use, but it can also indicate medication effects—or even a poor night's sleep.

82 Barbaux, L., Perrault, A. A., Cross, N. E., Weiner, O. M., Es-Sounni, M., Pomares, F. B., Tarelli, L., McCarthy, M., Maltezos, A., Smith, D., Gong, K., O'Byrne, J., Yue, V., Desrosiers, C., Clerc, D., Andriamampionona, F., Lussier, D., Gilbert, S., Tannenbaum, C., Gouin, J. P., … Dang-Vu, T. T. (2025). Effect of chronic benzodiazepine and benzodiazepine receptor agonist use on sleep architecture and brain oscillations in older adults with chronic insomnia. *Sleep*, 48(10), zsaf168. https://doi.org/10.1093/sleep/zsaf168

I think it does the field a disservice to make generalizations and grand assumptions about brain patterns. Computer tools and large-scale data analysis can help us start to make connections between physiological anomalies and brain patterns, but I think for the current state of the field, while qEEGs can detect atypical brain patterns, we need to test the body with other objective tests.

A qEEG should be the first test a provider runs when they see a new patient. In many cases, the qEEG will reveal a specific brain pattern, and the provider can use that pattern to *inform* the patient's treatment. They can make recommendations about medication, suggest changes to the person's environment, and recommend other modifications that the patient can make to reliably deal with their mental health concerns.

However, in the event that the qEEG *doesn't* show something amiss, the provider can start looking at other physiological, biological, environmental, or socioeconomic factors that are playing a role in the patient's symptoms.

One of the most remarkable and dramatic cases we had was with a patient who came to the clinic for psychosis. She had already been hospitalized numerous times and was not responding to antipsychotic medications or previous treatments.

I didn't personally know her history before conducting the qEEG analysis. So during the collaboration meeting with her mental health provider, I was surprised to hear her diagnosis because her scan looked normal. Obviously, the symptoms and the patient's distress were real: There was no way she would have driven across the country to the clinic on a whim. But in terms of her qEEG analysis, we couldn't find anything wrong and certainly nothing to indicate she was psychotic.

We recommended blood work with a focus on disease and immune markers. We found that she had a disproportionate amount of autoimmune antibodies targeting her brain tissue. These antibodies were also responsible for her infertility. So in essence, her body was attacking her brain which caused all of her symptoms as well as a host of other effects. Once we identified the root cause of her symptoms, we were able to offer treatment. Ironically, the treatment we used was more commonly applied in cancer and almost never used in psychiatry.

The patient rapidly got better after her treatment; so much so that, the last time we spoke, she had just given birth to a healthy baby.

What sticks with me about this patient is that if she had been treated purely as a psychiatric patient, she never would have gotten better. It was the fact that we *didn't* see atypical brain patterns that clued us in that this *wasn't* a mental health problem, but rather a physical one.

I do also want to stress here that the lack of an atypical qEEG result doesn't *always* mean there will be a biological basis for the mental health concern. We've had patients come in with serious mental health concerns such as suicidality or self-harm, and the qEEG results were typical and didn't show any of the brain patterns associated with these conditions.

When we tell the mental health providers about these patients, they will often run blood work, but at times, they may also delve deeper into the patient's environment. And often, this is where they uncover stories of abuse and trauma. In these cases, the qEEG can act like a gateway, where the provider can tell the patient, "From a biological standpoint, you shouldn't be suffering as much as you are; what else is going on?" And this gives patients the chance to understand that their struggles are not related to how their brain is wired (hardware), but rather caused by something external that they have been trying to keep a secret up until now (software).

For mental health providers, shifting from a symptoms-based approach that focuses almost exclusively on the mind to an objective approach that considers the entire body can be intimidating, but it's an essential step in getting more patients better, faster.

The best way to adjust is to start with the qEEG as the foundation. After you've had an interview with the patient about their symptoms, you can use the qEEG to inform their treatment and provide them with a more nuanced diagnosis. While you may have been able to diagnose a patient with ADHD based on an interview, the qEEG will help you narrow down the exact subtype of the diagnosis and, thus, the likely corresponding treatment.

Then if the treatment doesn't work, or the qEEG doesn't show any clear physiological explanation, you can start to ask questions which may further explain the patient's situation. That information can help you determine whether their environment is affecting them or if they have experienced trauma. You take out the guesswork that would normally occur from trying to treat a patient without all the necessary information, and you can test the body as well as the brain to get a more complete picture of what is going on.

Next, let's talk about how to approach testing the patient after you've done the qEEG.

Testing the Body

So what are the common tests to run after you get a qEEG result that doesn't explain the person's symptoms?

Starting with a general blood screening is a good idea to look at mineral levels, toxic exposure levels, and hormone levels that tend to cover most of the bases. If we suspect a gut-driven issue, we'll run food sensitivity tests, vitamin and mineral screeners, and check gut markers to make sure there are no pathogens lurking in the digestive tract.

Typical tests assess all major body systems and screens for kidney and liver function, immune function, hormone and nutritional deficiencies, and inflammation. Providers can use the patient's family history to guide them in choosing the initial tests to be run. While most blood screening tests are covered by insurance, some may require specialty labs with limited insurance billing.

Of course, testing is extremely situational, which is why it's so important to ask the right questions in addition to doing the test. A detailed intake can be invaluable at a later stage when you need more information. Plus, a more thorough intake can help you ask the right questions during the follow-up.

If providers want to shift towards testing the body, they will have to rethink their current methodology and orientation of their visits away from the subjectivity of the DSM. Currently, many providers deal primarily with acute cases: people in deep distress and mental health crises. A qEEG is very useful in these cases, as it can help the provider identify the problem and treatment rapidly without the need for guesswork and trial and error.

But getting a long-term resolution is where the whole-body model shines. Once the patient has gotten out of the acute phase, providers can conduct long-term work to identify potential underlying causes that medication can sometimes mask. Many patients want to get off their medications eventually, and this requires not only an understanding of their brain patterns, but also of their environment, potential biological factors, or history of trauma or abuse.

So for patients that want to do deeper work for their mental well-being, I'd say the qEEG is just the first step. The next is looking under the hood physiologically and seeing if there are any underlying conditions that might either create or exacerbate mental illness. And the final step is setting up a supportive environment and viewing the person's brain patterns as traits that can be either strengths or weaknesses.

This approach sets people up to succeed, not only in getting past their mental health crisis, but also toward thriving and living their best lives.

Summary

- Not all mental illnesses arise from brain dysfunction.
- Thyroid disease, allergies, abnormal lipid utilization, infections, and even vitamin deficiencies can cause mental health issues.
- An unremarkable qEEG test can hint at underlying physiological problems.
- Testing the whole body should start with a qEEG test first, then follow with physiological testing and finally evaluation of the person's environment.
- This type of whole-body approach in psychiatry can lead to long-term mental well-being.

Chapter 8
Lessons from Other Fields

Psychiatry doesn't exist in isolation. As we saw in Chapter 7, mental health is affected by more than just the brain. The patient's body, genetics, environment, and past experiences all play a huge role in their mental well-being. So psychiatry as a science can benefit from advances in other fields too. Medicines that target infections can alleviate psychotic episodes, and neurological brain tests like qEEG are proving invaluable as different fields team up to find the most effective psychiatric treatment for patients.

What Can Psychiatry Learn from Other Medical Fields?

In my experience, psychiatry often feels like it stands apart from other medical practices and can be more of an art than a science. Largely, this is because it tries to measure something considered intangible. Mental health issues are much harder to examine and diagnose than a broken bone or heart attack. At the moment, psychiatry relies more on a patient's perceived experience, which is why the DSM gained traction so easily:

It provided the illusion of being objective and scientific and of allowing psychiatry to appear more objective than it truly is.

But at its core, psychiatry is still a medical field. Objective testing through tools like the qEEG is possible, which means that the tenuous distinction between the fields is starting to shrink. That is precisely why it's time to ask what lessons can psychiatry learn from other medical fields, particularly those that rely heavily on patient self-reporting, and also what psychiatry can teach other fields.

"Subjective" Fields

If you ask a provider what the difference between neurology and psychiatry is, the answer will often be something like "One looks at the brain, the other looks at the mind." But what exactly is the mind? And where do conditions such as fibromyalgia, chronic Lyme disease, or chronic fatigue, which rely heavily on subjective patient self-reporting, fit in?

Ironically, a lot of these cases ended up in psychiatric offices. When providers see cases that are difficult to quantify and the treatments that would usually work in other cases don't, they will often send these types of patients off to psychiatrists, who have the reputation for being able to deal with so-called subjective diseases.

For the longest time, these patients were dismissed. Providers would think that either the patients were imagining the problem or looking for attention, particularly in cases where established treatments didn't work. Only with newer research are these previously neglected or dismissed conditions gaining traction and validity in the medical field.

Conditions like fibromyalgia were still hotly contested a few years ago, as some researchers refused to even acknowledge its existence. The problem is that a fibromyalgia diagnosis remains primarily clinical and relies on a patient's description of their symptoms (sound familiar?). But, a growing body of evidence shows that it has neurological causes, and MRIs show evidence of changes in the brain around pain receptors.[83] These objective tests are what have transformed fibromyalgia from a seemingly fake disease to a legitimate diagnosis.

So what lessons can psychiatry learn from this? There's a need for objective, biologically based tests and markers that can help with the diagnosis, treatment, and researching of the underlying causes of the psychiatric condition.

When I was in my residency training, we had a teenage girl come into the clinic for treatment. She had been diagnosed with seizures, but her treatments weren't working, and she wanted to finally learn how to drive. Before we could even run a qEEG, she had what she thought was a seizure in the office. And, when I saw this, my first question was, "Who said these are seizures? This isn't a seizure; this is a tic."

In response, we did a workup, and tested her for PANDAS—a streptococcal infection that can produce symptoms that are similar to mental health conditions such as tics and OCD. And with confirmation from the treatment response, lo and behold, that's what it was. But she had been written off in the neurology world because she wasn't responding to anti-epileptics.

---

83 Sluka, K. A., & Clauw, D. J. (2016). Neurobiology of fibromyalgia and chronic widespread pain. *Neuroscience*, 338:114–129.

It's only thanks to biomarkers and testing that we were able to find an abnormality, treat the abnormality, and help her get to drive to school and live happily ever after.

But I think that whenever we can't take precise measurements for specific symptoms, it's easy for the patient to get dismissed and written off, because the interaction between bacterial infection and psychiatric symptoms is so rare in physical medicine. However, in psychiatry, where looking at subjective information is the gold-standard method of diagnosis, providers have to take patients' experiences as truth. The focus on subjective experiences of physical symptoms is why psychiatry gets all these fringe cases that cannot be explained by traditional medicine, such as PANDAS, fibromyalgia, and chronic Lyme disease.

"Objective" Fields

There are several objective medical fields that stand out to me as examples of how psychiatry could function in the future. The first is cardiology. It's a tangible medical science, and heart issues affect many people in the US. No cardiologist would ever treat a patient purely symptomatically; if you come into the emergency room with chest pain, they'll do a short intake interview, but the bulk of testing is physical, including electrocardiograms (EKGs), X-rays, or blood work.

Imagine being a doctor and trying to diagnose a patient simply on the basis of them saying, "My chest hurts and my left arm is numb." While that may be enough information to guide you to certain tests, it's not enough to confirm a diagnosis of a heart attack. They could be having an anxiety attack, or they may have a pinched nerve combined with angina. You won't know until you test the patient physically, and you wouldn't start treatment until you're certain of the diagnosis.

An example of this idea is a young man who came to our clinic for Treatment Resistant-Depression (TRD). He was 28, hadn't had a job for three years, and couldn't even get out of bed. He didn't have any hobbies either and was reaching his breaking point.

Interestingly, after running a qEEG analysis, we couldn't detect any typical depression patterns. He did have significant markers more associated with ADHD along with some markers that pointed to slow processing, which we often see in people with head injuries.

Based only on his symptoms, it's easy to see why he was diagnosed with depression. Any checklist or interview would come to the same conclusion. But, without looking at the root cause, you wouldn't have any idea of what's going on with this man at all.

Once we identified the underlying cause—a head injury—we were able to prescribe treatments that would alleviate his symptoms. However, it took an objective test to get to that point; relying only on his symptoms had wasted years of his life on SSRIs and other drugs that simply couldn't work.

Oncology is another field that used to rely on polypharmacy or drugs that targeted any fast-growing cells. Tumors were all treated in similar ways, often with a combination of tumor removal and aggressive chemotherapy. This less-targeted approach didn't often work, and drugs that were nonspecific produced horrendous side effects including severe nausea and hair loss. And worse, trying a treatment that didn't work meant that the cancer could spread to other parts of the body. Through this lack of specificity of cancer treatment approaches, the medical community learned that not getting it right the first time could be *deadly* for the patient.

One major shift in cancer research came from the realization that lung cancer isn't a single condition, just as depression isn't a single condition. Individual cancer types have unique genetic markers that respond differently to treatment; for example, the treatment for triple-negative breast cancer will differ to that of inflammatory breast cancer.

This is similar, in some ways, to the heterogeneity found in mental health conditions. A depression diagnosis doesn't tell you at all which treatment is going to be effective. And the longer it takes you to find the right treatment, the more likely it is that the patient will suffer and potentially give up.

Cancer research has advanced dramatically both in diagnosis and treatment. Genetic testing and biomarkers can help oncologists pinpoint the exact type of cancer, the stage at which it's at, and the appropriate treatment. In the modern medical world, treatments have also become more specific; they no longer target every cell in the body, but they can hone in on target cancer cells. This means that treatment plans are not only more effective, but the drugs used within them have fewer side effects than older drugs.

This more targeted approach is exactly what we're trying to do with qEEG, ensuring that every person's treatment is tailored to their brain patterns instead of solely to their symptoms.

Psychiatry can also learn a lot from medicine's focus on prevention being better than cure and the use of tests that have predictive capacity to catch diseases early. Whenever you go to your doctor for an annual checkup, they're going to take your blood pressure and run a few simple blood tests before even interviewing you.

These tests are essential for picking up afflictions referred to as silent killers like diabetes and hypertension. In a lot of cases, these conditions can be asymptomatic for many years before suddenly becoming a crisis. Routine predictive testing can catch these conditions in the early phases, allowing the patient to make the necessary lifestyle changes to head off the disease before it starts.

The same could apply to psychiatry. A qEEG analysis can reveal underlying patterns that, depending on the patients' environment and lifestyle, can cause mental health concerns. By detecting these patterns early, providers could advise patients on ways they can avoid making their problems worse, either through lifestyle changes, medication, or a combination of the two.

Most self-harm questionnaires consist of very basic, impersonal questions that can come across as cold. Combined with the fact that self-harm still has a strong social stigma, many patients who self-harm may not answer such questionnaires truthfully.

In our research, qEEG can reveal self-harm markers, telling the story of what's going on in the patient's mind without the need for impersonal, unreliable tests.

A preventative approach hugely benefits providers. Instead of running around putting out fires, providers would be able to spend more time with each patient, ensuring every patient has the right tools to *thrive*. Not only would providers feel like they have more useful information and advice to give, they'd have a higher treatment success rate, hopefully leading to less burnout and stress for providers.

This approach would also benefit patients. Instead of having to go through a mental health crisis to find out there's a problem, providers could head the crisis off at the pass. This would also allow patients to learn ways to turn their brain patterns into strengths. Instead of having to deal with ADHD, they could harness their creative potential while minimizing the challenges that come with the patterns associated with attention deficits.

The final lesson psychiatry could learn from other medical fields is to conduct follow-up testing. If you have cancer, you'll have regular tests to check whether the cancer has truly gone away. If you have hypertension, you'll receive regular blood pressure tests to make sure that the treatment is working.

Psychiatry doesn't work that way. It uses artistry to arrive at a treatment and then relies on the patient's subjective assessment of how they feel to determine whether the treatment has worked or not. Many patients will only see their psychiatrists when they need refills instead of having regular check-ins. As a result, there's very little objective data as to whether a treatment was successful or not.

What Other Medical Fields Can Learn from Psychiatry

So while it's clear that psychiatry has a lot to learn from other medical fields, the reverse is also true. Psychiatry has several unique strengths that aren't often found in medicine that would be beneficial for medical practice in general.

One of the things that really stands out to me about the interaction between a mental health provider and their patient is the close relationship that forms and the compassion and bedside manner that psychiatrists develop.

Professionals in psychiatry can make people feel safe and validated in a way that some other fields may not be able to. We all know the stereotype of the doctor that sees their patients as a walking collection of symptoms and tests, and this is not the approach that mental health providers take. They are much more likely to know everything there is to know about their patient: what their day-to-day environment looks like, what hobbies they have, their relationships, and their private concerns and triumphs.

And medicine, in general, would be better if more doctors took this approach. Patients are often very likely to keep information to themselves, and this information could be vital in securing a diagnosis faster, particularly in cases where there are multiple potential options. Even simply making patients feel safe and heard could improve their outcomes or, at the very least, their experience at a hospital or clinic.

Another thing that working in mental health has taught me is just how much suffering goes unseen and untreated. People are stoic. They don't like to share their pain. As mental health providers, we get to see that vulnerable side more often, and it's telling just how many people have troubles going on underneath the surface.

I often wonder if the same is true for medical problems: Just how many people are walking around with chronic pain or fatigue, and just don't feel that it's important enough to go see a doctor about? And also, I'm not sure if doctors understand how much psychological suffering is happening right under their noses and the role that plays in their patient's physical ailments, especially patients that suffer from conditions that don't get better, whether it's chronic neck pain, rashes, or even allergies, and how those ongoing conditions can translate to long-standing psychological stress.

If we're talking about what medicine could learn about my idealized, strength-based, objective testing form of psychiatry, I think the main goal would be to focus on a strength-based approach (what we've called the husky phenomenon). This is completely unique to psychiatry, whereas in other fields symptoms are almost universally seen as negatives. In the husky phenomenon, we view brain patterns as things that can affect people differently depending on their environment. This gives us the chance to adjust a person's environment and treatment to help them thrive, without completely suppressing the traits that make them unique.

Summary

- Psychiatry has long stood apart from other medical professions, largely due to its more symptoms-based approach.
- As objective testing via qEEG becomes more common, psychiatry can start to align more closely with traditional medicine.
- Psychiatry should also embrace its heterogenous nature and tailor treatments to the patient's unique test results.
- Medicine can also learn from psychiatry, particularly in regards to empathy and communication.

Chapter 9

Breaking Free from the DSM

The facade of DSM satisfaction is crumbling, and the evidence is everywhere once you know where to look.

Behind closed doors, psychiatrists admit they're frustrated with treatment failures. Therapists confess that they ignore diagnostic labels and treat the whole person anyway. Even insurance companies are quietly questioning why they're paying for multiple medications that don't work.

The most telling indicator isn't what providers say publicly; it's what they do when given alternatives. Every time we introduce qEEG analysis to a new practice, the same pattern emerges. Initial skepticism gives way to cautious testing with their most challenging cases. Within months, they're using it as a frontline assessment tool. Why? Because it works, and they can finally see results that match their expertise.

This shift isn't happening uniformly across all provider types, and that's actually accelerating the change. Therapists, for instance, have always been more skeptical of diagnostic labels. They instinctively want to treat the whole person—including their environment—instead of relying on a diagnosis that focuses on symptoms. These providers are natural allies in moving beyond the DSM framework.

However, even the groups that recognize the dangers of labels remain trapped in DSM-influenced thinking. When discussing difficult patients, providers still default to talking about mood disorders, depression, anxiety, and other symptoms-based categories. This shows just how pervasive DSM thinking has become and why breaking free requires more than good intentions.

But the momentum is building from unexpected places. The psychiatric establishment itself has begun questioning the DSM's scientific foundation.

In 2013, Thomas Insel, the then-director of the National Institute of Mental Health (NIMH), and his compatriots Professor Allen Frances and the author Gary Greenberg made waves when they published a blog post criticizing the DSM's scientific lack of validity. This was just ahead of the publication of the newest version of the DSM, the DSM-5, which was an iterative update of the DSM-IV.[84]

The bulk of their argument focused on the lack of a biological basis for the DSM's diagnostic categories and the lack of its integration with objective science. The result of this blog was that the NIMH stopped funding research projects based on

84 Insel, T. (2013). Transforming Diagnosis. *NIMH Director Blog Posts.* Available at https://psychrights.org/2013/130429NIMHTransformingDiagnosis.htm

DSM categories and started supporting projects that looked across categories or subdivided categories into heterogeneous groups.

This blog post cemented the idea that the DSM wasn't suitable for everything in psychiatry, which represented a dramatic shift in thinking in the psychiatric research community. It diverted the focus away from symptoms-based observations that generalized symptoms under various umbrellas, such as depression, anxiety, and so on.

But while this blog post sparked fierce debate about the strength of the notion of the DSM as psychiatry's bible, Insel made it very clear that his criticism of the DSM was mainly focused on research and that he still supported the DSM as a way to diagnose and treat patients.

While Insel may have not gone as far in his criticism as we do in this book, he laid the foundation for thinking about psychiatry as more than just symptom clusters. He says that using the DSM as a diagnostic tool is similar to diagnosing a heart attack based on the quality of the chest pain. Psychiatry needs to catch up with the rest of medicine, which has realized that basing treatment on symptoms alone is rarely the best choice.

The difference now is that providers are pushing further than Insel did. They're not just questioning the DSM for research; they're abandoning it for patient care. And they're seeing the results that prove them right.

The remainder of this chapter is a discussion of how I see psychiatry shifting away from the DSM. We'll also talk about the current state of psychiatry and people who are already starting to question the DSM. Finally, we'll discover potential challenges that can impede the shift away from the DSM. Then in the next chapter we'll discuss actionable points to address these challenges.

Practitioners Want Alternatives

Alternative frameworks have been emerging for years, proving that the DSM monopoly was never inevitable.

The DSM underwent a huge foundational shift between its second and third editions when it adopted a symptoms-based approach to diagnosing mental health disorders. This left a lot of mental health clinicians, particularly those interested in psychodynamics, in a challenging position. These clinicians didn't want to view their patients in terms of categorical diagnoses, and either had to deny the DSM or develop an alternative.

Psychodynamics is the branch of psychology that deals with the relationship between the conscious and unconscious mental forces and emotions that form a patient's personality and motivation.

Several well-known psychodynamic experts decided to write a supplement to the DSM, one which approaches the understanding of mental health conditions from a very different viewpoint. The Psychodynamic Diagnostic Manual (PDM) is an attempt to "characterize an individual's full range of functioning, the depth as well as the surface of emotional, cognitive, and social patterns" and is meant to be used to describe "what one is, rather than what one has."[85]

Instead of looking at a patient's symptoms exclusively, the PDM aims to get a deeper understanding of the patient, not only in terms of their experiences, but also their personality, their environment, and the situation that shapes their current mental health concerns. It's a more holistic approach and one that works well for patients whose treatment is perhaps more geared towards environmental changes than pharmaceutical interventions.

However, despite its completely different foundational approach, the PDM doesn't attempt to supplant the DSM as the bible of psychiatry. Instead, it acts as a complementary manual that aims to shift the focus from the symptoms onto the person themselves.

The PDM has challenged the DSM, highlighting the potential weakness of a symptoms-based approach and pointing out the importance of viewing patients as individual humans with integrated systems of emotions and social patterns. It also shifts back to the idea that mental health conditions are not due to a single cause, but rather stem from a complex combination of factors.

To a large extent, that's what we're also trying to do: to showcase that mental health conditions are a result of a complex of factors, not just a single cause. We do it from the biology and environmental side, while the PDM does it from the social, emotional, and mental side.

---

85 *Psychodynamic Diagnostic Manual*, First Edition, pg. 17.

The early adopters are no longer isolated pioneers; they're becoming a movement. These trailblazers come in and say, "The system isn't working; we need to find better ways to help our patients." They tend to be people working in integrative settings that examine both the psychological and physiological components of mental health conditions.

What's changed is that these early adopters are now demonstrating measurable success that other providers can't ignore. Their willingness to challenge conventional wisdom isn't just setting the stage for change; it's proving that change works. And as word spreads through professional networks, the trickle of interest is becoming a flood of adoption.

Adoption of qEEG is Accelerating

The pattern of adoption is becoming predictable, and it's speeding up. What used to take months of convincing now happens in weeks. Providers who once dismissed objective testing are now asking how quickly they can implement it. The shift follows a clear trajectory that we've witnessed across hundreds of practices.

It starts with results they can't ignore. A colleague mentions their 90% success rate with treatment-resistant patients. A conference presentation shows brain scans that perfectly predict medication response. A frustrated provider finally gets a patient better by using qEEG-guided therapy after years of failed treatments.

The conversion happens fast once they try it. Within their first few cases, providers see patterns they never noticed before.

Brain scans reveal why certain patients never responded to SSRIs, why others had paradoxical reactions to stimulants, and why traditional therapy approaches failed. The data doesn't lie, and the results speak for themselves.

Then comes the cascade effect. Success with challenging cases builds confidence. Patient satisfaction scores jump. Word spreads through professional networks. Other providers start asking questions. What began as skeptical experimentation becomes standard practice.

We're seeing this acceleration across entire regional networks. One successful clinic influences referring physicians. Medical directors take notice of outcome improvements. Insurance companies start asking why other providers aren't achieving similar results. The competitive pressure becomes undeniable.

The adoption curve has hit its inflection point. Early majority providers, the pragmatists who wait for proven results, are now coming on board. They've watched the early adopters for years, seen the data, and recognized that objective testing isn't experimental anymore. It's simply better medicine.

How Objective Testing Will Finally Lay the DSM to Rest

One analogy that I keep coming back to when thinking about psychiatry is that of the blindfolded people and the elephant. Each person is feeling a different part of the elephant, which means that one is convinced they're tugging on a rope, while the other is convinced they're hugging a tree. And they can't reach a consensus so each is convinced the other is wrong because they're relying on their subjective experience rather than complete objective data. In their blindfolded state, they can't get a clear picture of what's really right in front of them.

I believe that objective testing will be like that moment of realization that happens when the blindfolded people take a step back and remove the blindfold to get a glimpse of the whole picture. That's when they'll have objective data that they can use to put their individual experiences into a larger perspective.

Integrative medicine is already on this path. Medical conditions can often show up as psychiatric conditions. For example, thyroid disorders manifest as deep depression, seizures manifest as hallucinations, and infections manifest as psychosis.

The unfortunate thing is that, for most patients, they'll only be presented with the option for an objective test when *all other options* have been exhausted. But when they do, they will finally see the elephant for what it really is, and they can finally progress onto effective treatment.

I expect that qEEG is going to start a snowball effect, allowing providers and patients to experience the benefits of objective testing with relatively low risks and low expense. And once people see the benefits of objective testing, momentum towards qEEG and other tests will start to build.

Challenges Facing the Break Away From the DSM

Breaking away from a way of thinking that is established and still considered reputable is never easy, particularly one as enshrined as the DSM. Understanding the challenges is the first step in starting to shift the perspective for the whole psychiatric field, and that's what we'll cover in this section. Then, in Chapter 10, we'll discuss what we're doing and what you can do to overcome these challenges and make mental health care more reliable for a wider range of people.

Friction from Providers

In general, many mental health providers don't see a problem with the current state of things as they stand. They think that the DSM works, that they serve their patients well, and that any problems have to do with the imprecision of single treatment options which can be fixed through a cocktail of medications. They've also been burned by new theories being debunked, such as neurotransmitter imbalances being the cause of mental health issues as diverse as schizophrenia, suicidality, and depression.

This gives them two very good (in their minds) reasons to be skeptical about tests like qEEG analysis. They might say, "If the system works, why change it? And if it doesn't, can you prove that your system works?"

Mental health is also a field that has a deep distrust of technology. Many therapists will still use paper and pen to record their sessions, despite having more efficient tools at their disposal. If you go into a high-end, cutting-edge medical clinic, you'll be confronted with clean glass and high-tech equipment as far as the eye can see. Whereas if you walk into many mental health centers, you'll get carpet, comfy couches, and decor from the '80s.

The distrust providers have for technology extends, obviously, to AI. And since a lot of what we do relies on data processing and AI, that can hurt qEEG's chance at credibility in psychiatry, especially since AI is rapidly becoming cast as a villain in some threatened circles. Some providers feel threatened by AI, worried that it will replace them, and so they are reluctant to listen to anything that has even a hint of the technology behind it.

There are several ways to lessen the skepticism facing qEEG and other objective psychiatric tests, despite their seemingly high-tech nature. The first would be to remind providers that EEG is an old technology and that all we're doing is putting it to new, practical use. Another way would be if insurance providers backed the technology, which would give qEEG and other objective tests the credibility they need in the eyes of providers and patients alike.

Lack of Insurer Buy-In

Currently, many health insurance companies don't cover qEEG as a test for mental health conditions. Being covered by insurance lends a certain credibility to a treatment or test, and lack of insurance has the opposite effect; many people will think, "If it isn't covered by insurance, it's bogus".

Insurance-based providers are going to have a hard time explaining to their patients why they need to pay out of pocket for a test, leading to a reluctance to offer the test in the first place. As someone who is familiar with qEEG technology, I can personally give enough reasons to pay out of pocket such as, "Doing this test will reduce the amount of medications you take, reduce the trial and error we have to go through, and help get you the assistance you need faster. It may even reduce your reliance on medication entirely." But a provider that doesn't know what to say can't easily communicate why the test would be beneficial to the patient. And so, they simply won't offer the test.

Public demand is likely going to be a huge driver in changing this, but it's a chicken-and-egg situation. The cycle looks something like this: If the insurance companies don't cover it, the providers won't offer it. Without provider adoption, insurers won't have any demand for the test; so they won't cover it. We need an external force to come in and drive demand, breaking that cycle.

Standardization

One of the reasons that insurance buy-in may be tricky is because, currently, there are many different ways to process a qEEG test, and the outputs aren't all compatible with each other. That means that someone can read about qEEGs like we do in our partner clinics and go to a qEEG clinic in their local area and get a completely different analysis or output, making it difficult or impossible to map out a reliable treatment plan. They might also find that their provider doesn't have the means to match patients to medication or the right lifestyle support. This doesn't really create confidence with providers, patients, or insurance companies!

There needs to be a uniformity to both how the test is run and how we match people to treatments. And, because qEEG testing for mental health is still in its infancy, we're just not there yet, a problem that is exacerbated by the diverse ways that providers want to conduct qEEG. A large part of the problem is the divide between providers who want to use normative databases and those that feel they're not the best tool for the job of treating mental health patients.

Reliance on Normative Databases

One of the biggest questions around standardization will be whether to use or avoid normative databases. These databases contain huge amounts of qEEG information, in theory obtained from a normal population and people who do not have mental health concerns.

The idea is that by comparing a patient's qEEG results to a normative database, providers can quickly identify which markers or patterns are out of range or abnormal. Unfortunately, while the theory sounds good, there are big issues surrounding normative databases (which we touched on briefly earlier in the book).

For instance, how are people chosen to be part of the database? What qualifies as normal, and what are the exclusion criteria? From our experience, we know that people can have abnormal ADHD markers, but because they are supported by their environment, they aren't diagnosed with ADHD or display any symptoms. These people may be included in a normative database because they don't have an ADHD diagnosis, despite the fact that their ADHD patterns are, to put it bluntly, not normal at all.

Secondly, we're not sure how stable many of these markers are. We've spent years finding biomarkers that are stable, ones that don't fluctuate much based on a patient's mood, what they had for breakfast that morning, their sleep, and so on. But we can't be sure that the normative databases have done the same.

For these reasons, in our analysis we stay away from normative databases and rely instead on markers that have been identified in scientific studies that correlate to certain characteristics. And since this choice has such a huge impact on the how the test is conducted and the markers that are examined, it's something that we need to resolve and standardize if qEEG is going to become a viable alternative to the DSM.

And while it's likely that the shift away from the DSM towards objective testing is going to happen sometime in the future, there are things that can speed up the process.

Accelerating the Shift

While I suspect that the shift away from the DSM is inevitable, the slow pace of change means that patients are being subjected to all the issues we've described in this book. There are two fundamental components that are necessary to accelerate the shift that aren't, unfortunately, in anyone's control.

In Chapter 10, we'll take a deeper look at what you can do to accelerate the shift, as a provider, patient, qEEG clinician, or researcher. In the meantime, here are a few examples.

Insurance Reimbursement

Shifting away from the DSM would be a game changer in terms of insurance reimbursement. It could help overcome provider reluctance because it would both validate qEEG as a legitimate test and create a financial incentive for providers to offer it.

Once they tried it and saw how effective it was in predicting treatment outcomes, they'd do it more, increasing demand and creating a snowball effect.

Training and Knowledge-Building

At the moment, we're still at the point where qEEG isn't standardized, and this applies to aspects of the testing process such as interpreting results as well. You could go to three providers with the same qEEG result and they probably might agree on the base aspects, but not the nuances. It's important to get everyone in the field reasonably aligned. Doing so will require extensive training and certification. It's also why we offer a complete service that includes interpretation so providers don't need to read the qEEG maps and can instead focus on what the results mean for their patients.

Moving away from the DSM isn't going to be easy. Providers tend to be deeply entrenched in the type of thinking promoted by the DSM and are skeptical of new developments in psychiatry. Objective tests are the key to this shift, offering many varied benefits to patients and providers while also promoting a biology-based approach to psychiatry. The challenges facing the shift are diverse and systemic, and it is my strong belief that we—patients, providers, and qEEG clinicians—need to come together, overcome the challenges facing us and herald a new, more effective approach to psychiatry.

Summary

- Currently, providers may not know about the problems with the DSM and subjective diagnosis and treatment.

- However, trailblazers are starting to notice the cracks and vocalize their concerns.
- The biggest challenge facing the shift away from the DSM is a combination of provider skepticism and a lack of knowledge.
- Other challenges include a lack of insurer buy-in, lack of standardization in qEEG analysis, and the use of normative databases which can skew results.
- Accelerating the shift away from the DSM requires insurers to cover objective testing, and at the same time, the industry needs better training for providers and qEEG practitioners.

Chapter 10

Empowering Patients and Providers

Challenging any idea that is deeply entrenched requires a multifaceted approach. One group acting alone won't change much. Providers won't take qEEG seriously until the field is standardized to some extent, and patients won't know to ask for qEEG until they're recommended by providers. And the pressure from providers will then encourage qEEG clinicians to get their houses in order regarding standardized best practices. But what helpful approaches can we take in the meantime?

The previous chapter looked at the biggest challenges facing the shift towards objective-based testing. In this chapter, we'll look at what providers, patients, and qEEG clinicians can do to turn the tide and provide better mental health care.

What Can Providers Do?

Providers have a vital role in the way psychiatry is practiced and are key to shifting the field away from subjective, symptoms-based practices. If you've made it this far into the book, you should have a clear idea of the drawbacks of the DSM and the benefits that qEEG and other objective tests could offer. But knowing these things and implementing the changes I'm suggesting are two very different things. Here's how I would recommend mental health providers start incorporating qEEG into their practice.

Start Using qEEG

The simplest and most obvious action is to simply start requesting qEEG analyses for patients. Just using qEEG can start the snowball effect of moving psychiatry towards objective testing. It signals to insurance companies that there is a medical interest in qEEG and other tests. It also signals to patients that objective testing is a viable alternative to diagnosing along DSM categories and has many benefits, which are outlined in the book. Finally, it signals to qEEG providers that they need to get their act together by standardizing qEEG analysis for psychiatry if they want to get more business.

These actions can require a bit of a learning curve especially for providers who have never used anything other than the DSM. A common misconception, though, is that the mental health provider should be the one doing all the testing and analysis, which is simply not true. A general practitioner doesn't spin blood samples, an oncologist doesn't spend time in tissue culture, and mental health providers don't need to conduct qEEG tests themselves.

The first step is providers recognizing that they need objective data and then finding qEEG clinicians who can give them this information—people who have made their careers out of providing this data. Mental health providers can then start integrating this data into their diagnostic and treatment flows, but without necessarily having to do the analysis themselves. They don't have to buy equipment. And they don't have to learn how to perform these tests. They just send the patient to the qEEG provider and get a report. I think that's the easiest way, and that's usually what turns a provider who uses our services regularly into a qEEG hero.

Providers can keep seeing the patients they're seeing and doing what they normally do, but then have this extra tool in their arsenal. They can use qEEG on treatment-resistant patients and patients who are on three or four medications or take a diagnosis-based approach where they focus on patients with ADHD or depression and expand from there. Providers that do this will also often start to collaborate with other providers in the region that are doing the same and eventually use qEEG as part of the default diagnostic plan for the practice.

Of course, a tricky thing is that many providers, once they start to see the value of qEEG, start thinking about getting the equipment and offering it to their patients themselves. It makes sense as a value-add; patients don't need to drive to another clinic and can get their test done in-house instead. However, really getting a handle of qEEG is almost like learning a completely new discipline, which is why we often recommend just using a third-party service instead. Let me explain.

Work with Board-Certified Professionals

Finding a good qEEG clinician can be challenging, especially as, at the moment, a qEEG practitioner doesn't need a formal certification or degree to conduct the test. This can muddy the waters and provide bad information.

It's important to find a qEEG analyst who has some form of medical background or a higher education qualification. You can also look at providers accredited with the International qEEG Certification Board (IQCB),[86] which ensures they are versed in the current best practices in the field, meaning they can offer a reasonable standard of service and analysis.

Unfortunately, finding the right qEEG analysis team can be intimidating. What many providers will find is that, currently, qEEG is a world of its own. There are several different certifications, like qEEG-D, qEEG-T, and qEEG-DL, so it can feel quite overwhelming to a mental health provider just looking to find a basic package. But finding a board-certified professional will still be much easier and more cost-effective than trying to conduct internal qEEG tests out of a mental health practice.

According to the IQCB website: The **qEEG-DL** certification is for individuals licensed in health care and certifies their ability to conduct and read a qEEG analysis. The **qEEG-T** certification is for technologists who are not licensed in health care, but can still conduct a qEEG analysis. The **qEEG-D** is the highest possible certification and represents someone who has a master's degree or higher, along with their certification in conducting and interpreting qEEG results. The **qEEG-DL** signifies that this individual is also licensed in their field.

86 https://qeegcertificationboard.org/

It also doesn't help that many organizations are doing their own thing and will have their particular niche. This is great if you have a patient that fits that niche, but can be frustrating if you're looking for an all-in-one type of solution.

This all-in-one solution is what our lab in Denver offers. We put all of these disparate elements together to assist providers with getting the information they need, without having to jump through hoops or learn a completely new discipline.

Talk About qEEG with Colleagues

One of the best ways to raise awareness quickly is at conventions and other research-oriented gatherings. While most providers simply want to do their job, there are those who love being at the forefront of their field, publishing case studies and pushing boundaries. And we need people who use qEEG in their own practices to present more about it.

Many of the providers that have come to our clinic do so because they heard about our service at a conference or from colleagues. And typically, they will conduct a qEEG on themselves because of something they're struggling with or use it on a family member. So many of the providers we work with have children that are struggling, and these providers saw the benefits of testing their children directly. But without that initial seed of knowledge about this type of analysis, they'd never think to even try something like qEEG.

A large part of using qEEG in the future starts with having the conversation about brain patterns within the context of mental health, especially mental health education. It doesn't do a whole lot of good to have a symptoms-based education and then a totally separate course on qEEG; the idea of objective testing needs to become embedded in the mental health curriculum.

But providers are only one piece of the puzzle. Another very powerful group of people who can influence the future of qEEG in mental health, and the transition away from the DSM, is the patients themselves.

What Can Patients Do?

Many patients feel disenfranchised about their health care, often thinking that they're at the whim of their providers. But while dealing with stubborn providers and outdated notions can be extremely frustrating, patient-led movements can be powerful, especially if they gain enough traction to find their way into state and federal legislatures.

Advocacy starts with patients asking for a qEEG test. It may not be simple or easy as many providers are stuck in their ways and don't see any problems with the DSM. But parents who don't want to medicate their children, patients who have tried all sorts of medication to no avail, or simply people who have been let down by the mental health care system should have the power to fight and advocate for objective testing and the benefits it brings.

And if your provider doesn't want to do a qEEG? Find one who is open to it.

The second part of advocacy is talking about the qEEG. Tell your friends, talk about it on podcasts, and share information about it on social media. Grassroots movements begin organically, and once they gain enough momentum, they can have a huge impact on establishments.. Organizations like the IQCB are more geared towards providers and training, but they do have resources about what qEEG is, how it works, and how it can be applied to psychiatry and mental health. These talking points can be invaluable for people wanting to spread the word.

Patient-led advocacy can often feel like an uphill struggle against established medical norms. People can be stigmatized and ostracized for their beliefs, even when they have clear evidence that these beliefs are valid. But while it's difficult to engage in this kind of advocacy, these movements—in combination with a bit of luck—often yield results. And hopefully, the same will be true for any patient-led movement promoting objective, biological testing for mental health conditions.

Lyme disease is a classic example of how patient-led movements can yield significant results. While the pathogen responsible for the disease has been known since 1981, the medical community has been split about its treatment and even its diagnosis. The problem is that the bacterium causing the disease is complex, with a multistage lifecycle consisting of several host-pathogen interactions. Even worse, the bacterium doesn't confine itself to one system; it can attack multiple systems in the body, leading to a confusing and sometimes contradictory set of results.

Chronic Lyme disease, which can persist for years after the initial infection, has been hotly contested, with many health care practitioners even denying its existence. Patients in the early 2000s formed support groups online to help other sufferers get the care they needed. These groups were also vocal about education and managed to petition their state legislatures to protect doctors who were willing to treat late-stage, or chronic, Lyme disease.[87]

These groups never gave up, despite increasing pressure from the medical community and stigmatization from their friends and families.

But even the most vocal patient-led movement can't succeed alone. In a surprising twist of fate, a group of researchers all contracted Lyme disease at once while on a field trip. This group then shifted its research focus and became the bridge between patients and the established medical world. And once the bridge was there, it took funding and a concerted effort between patients, academics, and doctors to finally get the research into Lyme disease started in the US.

Since those early initial stages, Lyme disease has become legitimized through research and provider case studies. But it took a spark, the patient-led initiative combined with a willingness to work with health care providers, legislators, and academics, to really solidify the reality that chronic Lyme disease exists and its sufferers deserve to be taken seriously.

What Can the qEEG Community Do?

Now that we've covered what providers and patients can do, let's look at one final group. Clinicians offering qEEG testing,

87 Sotsky J. (2022). Lyme Disease in Psychiatry: Controversies, Chronic Symptoms, and Recent Developments. *Psychiatric Times* (39)1.

technicians, and academics form the third leg of the triangle needed to cement qEEG in psychiatry. They are the foundation of the practice, and as such, often face the most severe challenges in promoting their field. There are a few different ways to address these challenges.

Standardization

The current biggest challenge facing qEEG as a psychiatric tool is the lack of standardization across the field, as discussed in detail in Chapter 9. This hurts the field in a number of ways, from making it difficult for mental health providers to find reputable qEEG clinicians to delegitimizing the field in the eyes of insurance companies, which in turn makes providers and patients reluctant to try it.

By this point in the book, you know that qEEG clinicians are the ones responsible for making the field legitimate and useful to health care providers and their patients. In terms of psychiatry, qEEG is still a relatively novel and untested methodology. It's going to require a concerted effort on the part of all clinicians to get to the nuts and bolts of what makes qEEG a useful tool. This includes actually figuring out which data matters and what that data says.

So how do we do that? Unfortunately, there isn't a simple answer. One aspect that needs careful consideration is what I call guru thinking. Each team currently seems to be fragmented, offering their own version of the truth. For instance, I was at a conference where a qEEG provider was asserting that a particular biomarker was associated with trauma, and all I could think was, *That's the loosest connection*

I've ever heard. That biomarker is also associated with anxiety and many other mental health conditions too.

The best way forward, in my opinion, is to get more research and more funding into the field so that the core truths shake out. Once we have research that we can point to saying, "This marker shows this; that one shows that," it would lead to less fragmentation and more cohesion, with consistent, predictable outcomes. Ultimately, as qEEG clinicians, we need to realize that this isn't about ego, and it's not about being seen as gurus, but rather, it's about helping patients get better.

Certification, Training, and Education

Organizations like the IQCB and Biofeedback Certification International Alliance (BCIA) are going a long way in standardizing and promoting qEEG as a psychiatric tool. Even for people who are experienced in qEEG analysis, the training and certification these organizations provide can help everyone align on best practices and keep updated on the latest research.

The IQCB actually published a set of guidelines in 2025 that tries to tackle some standardization aspects.[88] These guidelines focus on data acquisition, including artifact management, which has been a huge issue for many qEEG providers around the country. Even just standardizing this aspect of qEEG testing is beneficial for the field. It ensures that, no matter where you get your data from, it will be usable for subsequent analysis.

88 Collura, T., Cantor, D., et al. (2025). International QEEG certification board guideline minimum technical requirements for performing clinical quantitative electroencephalography. *Clinical EEG and Neuroscience*, 15500594241308654.

Now what we need is someone to go further, to offer high-quality training on every aspect of the qEEG analysis after data collection and establish and then share a consensus about which biomarkers to look for with regards to psychiatric diagnosis and treatment.

Education doesn't only have to extend to qEEG clinicians. In many cases we've had to educate mental health providers to shift them away from symptoms-based diagnosis to a more objective treatment. For example, we've had to tell them that, yes, depression is a diagnosis, but not all types of depression respond well to the same treatment. And qEEG can help differentiate between those subtypes and provide a valid treatment option.

The Use of Normative Databases

We've discussed the problem of normative databases several times in this book already. Briefly, normative databases are expected to offer a baseline of what a so-called normal brain should look like and tell a provider how much a patient deviates from those norms.

However, there are several issues with these databases; the biggest one being the selection criteria used. For instance, a normative database should not include anybody with mental health conditions but, as we've shown throughout the book, there are people who may have mental health markers that do not manifest mental health symptoms. These people would be included in a normative database, despite their markers being out of normal range.

While normative databases may be useful in fields such as neurotherapy, they are less useful in psychiatry. By focusing on symptoms and not the underlying brain patterns, normative databases tend to have a muddy foundation and may not offer much in terms of treatment predictability for mental health disorders.

If qEEG providers decide that they want to continue with normative databases, we need to decide on one database that all tests are compared to. Trying to use several databases just confuses the issue even more and adds unnecessary variability to the way we interpret results.

In my view, we need to steer clear of normative databases and instead focus on specific biomarkers associated with a particular presentation, one of which is that people who have a high theta/beta ratio tend to have attentional deficits and be more impulsive when in unsupportive environments. We will still, obviously, have a normal range, but we can base these on clinical findings that we obtain through our testing. So rather than comparing the patient to a whole normative database, we could look at individual brain patterns and published values of deviations and treatment response and compare them to other people who responded or didn't respond to treatments, which would be more clinically useful to providers and patients.

So now you're all fired up to bring qEEG to the masses, regardless of whether you're a mental health provider, patient, or qEEG clinician. Let's look at some resources that can help you set that change in motion.

Useful Resources to Learn More About qEEG

The International Society for Neuroregulation and Research (ISNR) is one of the best resources for research in this field, currently. In addition to its yearly conference, the society has a wide range of resources and educational tools, a bibliography, and a recommended reading list. Their website also has guidelines for practice. While not explicitly about qEEG, the society collaborates with the IQCB and can be valuable for finding qEEG providers in different areas.

The Association for Applied Psychophysiology and Biofeedback (AAPB) is an organization with a massive amount of published literature. In addition to its flagship journal, *Applied Psychophysiology and Biofeedback Journal*, the organization also publishes *Biofeedback*, a quarterly peer-reviewed journal. The website has an extensive range of webinar recordings and publications that start at the basics of biofeedback and build upon that foundation.

We've also started offering resources to providers, qEEG clinicians and patients. The most accessible one is the *Off-Label* podcast which explores a lot of the themes raised in this book in a clinical and real-world context. We try to cover various topics that apply to a lot of patients, but the podcast also has useful information for providers looking for something more practical than research articles.

Our website also has many articles spanning most topics in clinical practice from predicting violent aggression to suicide and substance abuse and contact details for providers who want to start checking out the benefits of qEEG for themselves.

Summary

- Making qEEG more commonplace and shifting away from the DSM will require a multipronged approach.
- Mental health providers can get the ball rolling by requesting qEEG tests for treatment-resistant patients from a certified qEEG provider. Some providers even try qEEG on themselves first.
- These providers can also then spread the work through conversations at conferences and informal chats with colleagues.
- Patients have a lot of power to push for objective testing in psychiatry.
- Advocacy and pressure can shift well-established practices, but they need to align with academic and medical professionals too.
- The qEEG world in general needs to standardize its messaging and practices.
- Professional boards focused on promoting qEEG are vital in this aspect as well as in providing training and education.

Chapter 11

The Future of Mental Health

As a qEEG provider that has worked with tens of thousands of patients and personally reviewed and reported on nearly 50,000 scans (I've lost count, frankly) over the past few years, I firmly believe that qEEG and objective testing is the future of mental health. I have seen so many patients transformed by such a simple procedure that I don't understand how anyone wouldn't want to use it.

A few key stories have stuck with me over the years, ones that best illustrate the power of qEEG:

The first is of a middle-school aged boy being treated for ADHD. His parents were just about to move him to another school halfway across the country to help him deal with his symptoms. After a qEEG, we noticed that he had a particular marker that was positively affected by a medication commonly used as an anti-epileptic, but not often used in ADHD treatments. Matching the treatment to the boy's patterns, rather than his symptoms, meant that we chose a non-standard option, and it paid off. The medication transformed his life; he was able to stay at home and excel at school. This happened all because we trusted the process and treated the pattern instead of the symptom.

The second is a woman in her mid-30s who was struggling with depression and anxiety. She was unsatisfied with her job and had gone through three career changes in three years trying to find her niche. When we tested her, we saw that she had a pattern associated with deficits in social cognitive processing abilities (social skills). Not only did the result validate her experience, but it also gave her the chance to understand her deeper needs. We didn't even change her medication, just helped her change her environment to better suit her traits. Since then, she's found a career she loves, and she's satisfied with the outcomes we were able to help her achieve in her life—so much so that she still checks in occasionally to tell us how she's doing.

Finally, we also helped an older gentleman who had struggled with depression his entire life. He had tried behavioral therapies, medication, and even psychedelics, but nothing seemed to help. We noticed that he had a particular brain pattern, a mu rhythm, that responded positively to oxytocin, the feel-good chemical. Despite this being completely unheard of as a depression treatment at the time, we treated him with oxytocin and the change was almost immediate. Again, by treating the pattern and not the symptom, we had transformed his life. I often wonder what would have happened if he had received this treatment 20 or 30 years ago rather than during the twilight of his life.

All of these stories show us what mental health *could* be like if we stepped away from the current model. And while we have a long road ahead of us, I'm still hopeful that big changes are on the horizon and that they will benefit patients, providers, and everyone in the mental health space.

I don't expect the road ahead to be completely smooth sailing. But based on what I've seen happening in the mental health field in terms of qEEG and objective testing, I like to envisage a timeline of how I expect the mental health world to look like at various points in the future.

One Year From Now

I think in the near future, there's going to be more interest around novel treatments. Previously unthinkable treatments, like psychedelics, are becoming more accepted, and I think qEEG can lead the transformation towards a new way of thinking where these other novel treatments (if they work) can also become accepted.

I suspect that qEEG is also going to get a lot more attention from people who want to improve their performance, including the type of people who want to optimize when they should sleep, what type of foods they should eat at certain points in the day, and so on. I can see how something like neurotherapies, where qEEG is used in real time to train the brain into certain patterns, could be like catnip to these performance enhancers. And since neurofeedback and qEEG are almost interchangeable in the common consciousness, as these performance influencers start picking up on qEEG, it will become more common on social media and get more traction among patients. Of course, we should consider the pseudoscience aspect of influencers: that many of the trends they latch onto have no credible basis whatsoever (such as all-meat diets, microsleeping, and so on). I think providers need to get ready to address this possibility.

In my ideal world, the next year will shine a spotlight on qEEG's predictive capability in suicidality. It's something we've worked on for years and have published on too. We need to do more work in this area, and with support from government, schools, law enforcement organizations, and other groups, we can expand and validate our findings and showcase our high degree of predictability. It's something that has an immediate impact and can save lives.

Five Years From Now

I'm hoping that in the next five years, qEEG will have universal coverage from third-party payers. This will take a lot of work, unifying certifications and training, coming up with best practices, and so on, but I think it's achievable.

I think more common use of qEEG will also encourage a shift towards models where it's normal for people to talk about their brain patterns rather than a DSM diagnosis. They might say they have a high theta/beta ratio rather than sharing they have ADHD. Instead of talking about anxiety and depression, we could talk about an underarousal that can be addressed by more stimulation to support that need, rather than a medication that works to suppress the symptom.

Ten Years From Now

I expect that the field of qEEG will explode in the next ten years as we continue to move away from the DSM. There will be a lot more research and more nuance in what we can achieve with qEEG, and I expect there may be other objective tests also coming to light at this point.

As research into qEEG matures, we'll have a more refined view of how various patterns interact with each other and what it means for patient treatments. At the moment, we don't need more treatment options; we need more accurate diagnostic tools to guide providers towards the right, *targeted* treatments when they're suitable.

Our current objective tests, like qEEG, are probably not the endpoint of the shift away from the DSM and the transformation of psychiatry. I'm almost certain that something even more refined, accurate, and simple to use will be developed in the next ten years, but we always need to remember that it started with qEEG.

Will psychiatry have moved away from the DSM completely within ten years? It's hard to say, but at the very least, I think psychiatry will have a more biology-based approach than it does now. The criticisms of the DSM have been piling up, people have been offering alternatives, and the objective testing approach is starting to gain traction. But considering how entrenched the DSM language is, both in psychiatry and the outside world, as long as providers put labels on patients, I can't imagine it will go completely away.

Ideally, psychiatry will catch up to modern medicine, where it has to be precise, it has to be objective, and it has to be biologically based. We don't need to reinvent the whole system and we don't need to find new treatments. All we need to do is refine our tools and approach and understand that using the correct tools *accurately* will do more to benefit patients and providers than any new treatment or device. And that's where qEEG and other objective tests will shine.

Conclusion

In my ideal future, qEEG is a commonly used tool to help people to understand their brain patterns better. This understanding can help resolve the husky phenomenon —where a person's environment can determine how their patterns manifest—and lead to a place where people don't struggle to fit their basic patterns to complex environments. Instead, people will have the knowledge and power to fit their environment to their brain pattern, leading to people thriving, no matter how challenging their patterns may be.

Getting to this future isn't going to be easy. It's going to need a combination of luck and planning from a host of different people, including qEEG clinicians and researchers, mental health providers, patients, legislators, and health insurance providers. But, considering the current state of mental health in the US, and the sheer number of people affected by the guessing game providers are forced to play, shaping a future that is focused more on objective testing is well worth the effort.

Current psychiatry is a gamble, and I firmly believe that qEEG can help providers and patients ensure the odds are in their favor.

About the Author

Dr. Steven Rondeau ND, BCN(EEG), qEEG-DL, is a Licensed Naturopathic Doctor and the founder and president of Axon EEG Solutions. His unconventional entry into mental health was unintentional, and perhaps that's exactly what the field needed.

As a father and husband, Dr. Rondeau brings personal urgency to his work, driven by a fundamental belief that differences in mental health are not pathology but strengths that should be supported rather than pathologized. Just as we recognize that a husky struggles in the desert but thrives in the snow, Dr. Rondeau applies this same principle to human neurodiversity. The challenge has been that we don't have the playbook yet, but that's what his work is changing

Dr. Rondeau completed his medical training at Southwest College of Naturopathic Medicine in Phoenix, AZ, where he first discovered the predictive potential of qEEG technology. While still in medical school, he achieved board certification in qEEG and was recruited to serve as adjunct faculty in the mind-body department.

After graduation, Dr. Rondeau pioneered the first developmental pediatric naturopathic residency program in the country. It was during this residency work that his revolutionary approach to brain-based medicine began to emerge, focused on understanding individual brain patterns and creating environmental supports rather than forcing conformity to normal stereotypes.

Dr. Rondeau's most significant contribution thus far has been the creation of EEGDataHub.com, a revolutionary platform housing one of the world's largest human brain data repositories. As an early adopter of AI in mental health, he developed this proprietary database to enable precision treatment guidance for individuals of all ages based on objective biomarkers rather than the traditional DSM framework. In 2022, this pioneering work earned the prestigious AAMP award for medical innovation.

Dr. Rondeau has authored multiple peer-reviewed papers on objective brain testing utilizing qEEG, including research on suicide prediction and systematic challenges to the DSM.

Based in Colorado but frequently traveling worldwide with his family, Dr. Rondeau is driven by a vision of preventing suicide, despair, and hopelessness in individuals who are too often labeled treatment-resistant or dismissed for not fitting societal norms. He argues that as a society we should demand more of our mental health systems than trial and error. His work and this book are intended to serve as the much-needed owner's manual for a more precise and compassionate approach to mental health care.

Acknowledgements

This work would not have been possible without the support and collaboration of many incredible people who have shaped both the journey and the mission.

To the early providers and healing centers who believed in our vision when we were just getting started. A special thanks to the amazing team at Wholeness Center in Colorado for supporting our early work. Your faith made everything that followed possible.

To the remarkable team at Axon EEG Solutions who built the most sophisticated brain data processing platform in the world, especially our software development team. Thank you for the countless late nights and early morning meetings, which have turned complex ideas into solutions that change lives.

To our consultants and team members along the way, each bringing expertise that has strengthened our approach and enriched our understanding.

To the parents and patients who have trusted us with their stories and allowed us to learn alongside them, including those families we've lost along the way. Your experiences continue to drive our determination to find better answers.

To Ania, whose editorial collaboration helped transform years of clinical work into the book you're holding.

To our publishing team and editors for their dedication in bringing this work to life.

And to our partner providers who advance this mission daily. You are changing mental health care one patient at a time.

www.ingramcontent.com/pod-product-compliance
Lightning Source LLC
Chambersburg PA
CBHW071443230926
51846CB00001B/319
* 9 7 8 1 9 6 7 5 8 7 6 6 7 *